HERE IS JESUS

40 EASY BIBLE STUDIES FOR THE GOSPEL OF MARK

PAUL M. HARPER

Ark House Press
arkhousepress.com

Cataloguing in Publication Data:
Title: Here is Jesus
ISBN: 978-1-7643820-9-0 (pbk)
Subjects: REL006800 RELIGION / Biblical Commentary / New Testament / Jesus, the Gospels & Acts; REL006710 RELIGION / Biblical Studies / New Testament / Jesus, the Gospels & Acts; REL067040 RELIGION / Christian Theology / Christology.

Cover photo is upon The Sea of Galilee, taken during a Ridley College Study Tour, 2018

Design by initiateagency.com

In memory of David Williams, Lecturer at Ridley Theological College, who taught Greek and New Testament when I was there in the '90's. His love of the Gospels was inspiring. He always referred to himself as 'a simple Bible-believing Christian'.

CONTENTS

INTRODUCTION

After 30 years of Bible ministry in one way or another, I thought it was time to get these studies on Mark published. This set of studies has been used in many different locations and settings, beginning with the initial prompting from a wise mentor, a prolific preacher and teacher in Melbourne, Australia. Whether it be a small group huddled in an apartment in Carlton, or a family in a home in Mulgrave, or a mother reading while she does housework in Ballarat, these studies have proven effective in bringing people closer to Jesus.

Through the many ups and downs of life, where distractions abound and stresses squeeze us for time and energy, we can lose our way, become discouraged. We are all lost, at the mercy of this evil world of mankind and the Devil. One person can keep us on track; one person can rescue us and relieve our burdens, Jesus the Saviour of the world. In our time and age God's word has been available for all to read in our own language for 500 years. I grew up in a Roman Catholic home, where any real teaching of the Bible only came about long after the Second Vatican Council of 1965. It had little effect on my family or school life which was strict and harsh. Only at age 28 did the glorious truth of the Gospel, the love of God, shine in on my life, through extraordinary means. The impact this had on my past experience as a Catholic brought about a sense of disappointment, feelings of grief, that the Good News had been kept hidden from me for so long. The ongoing effect has spurred me on to open up God's wonderful word in the most straightforward way possible, for people who desperately need it.

The focal point in Mark is the last miracle, just before the final events; the healing of a blind man at the end of chapter 10. He calls out to Jesus, for mercy. Jesus hears him and asks what he wants. "Rabbi, I want to see." The first thing he sees is Jesus, who encourages him, "Go, your faith has healed you." And then he followed Jesus. It's as simple as that. Do you want to see Jesus? Mark's portrayal is crystal clear.

In a nutshell, what is Christianity about? It's about Jesus, the Son of God, coming into this world to save us from sin and evil, and give us new life, eternal life. But how can I receive all this great stuff from God, and how can I know it's true, anyway?

The answer is there are two things you can do:

1) Pray to God that he himself will speak to you; and
2) Read God's word in the Bible.

It's only when a person has come to that point in their life where they are *open* to God, when they realize this world is not all that it's cracked up to be (especially on T.V. and social media), that a person is in a position to *hear* God, to give him a go and listen to what he has to say.

I am excited about Mark's Gospel because it's a great place for anyone who wants to get started investigating Christianity. It's also good for those of us who have been Christians for a short time or a long time, to refresh and clarify and build up the foundation of our faith. Mark's account is the shortest and most 'uncluttered' when compared to the accounts of Matthew, Luke and John. This makes it powerful indeed, focusing on the most important things.

What should you expect, from reading Mark's Gospel and doing these studies? First and foremost you should *get to know Jesus* (or get to know him better). Christianity is not a religion of rules and ceremonies but is rather a real and living *relationship* with Jesus Christ. In Mark's Gospel you will see what Jesus did, you will hear what he said and taught, and you will gain an understanding about his purpose and mission in his life, death and resurrection. But you are not just reading history; this Jesus Christ you read about will be present with you as you read, because he is the living Lord of the universe now. He knows you, he knows exactly what's happening in your life now, and he's right with you in a real spiritual way, making these words come to life. He will speak directly to your heart, if you are open to him.

I hope you see that my purpose in writing these studies, therefore, is not that you will believe what *I* say, or follow *me*, but that you would see *Jesus*, through God's word in the Bible. This is the heart of Christianity. My words are only here to help you open up the word of God a bit, to help you understand it. (After all, it was written nearly 2,000 years ago). With this in mind, I normally prefer people to do these studies in a group, where you can all read the passage together and then make your *own* observations and ask questions *before* reading my notes. Time and again I am impressed by how perceptive people can be, even if it is the first time they have read the Bible. You see, I want to give people confidence that God's word is not so far removed from us that we can't understand a large proportion of it for ourselves. Great things have happened in the world over the last 2,000 years, when people have started reading God's word for themselves.

So if you are reading these studies alone by yourself, or in preparation for a study group, please follow these steps:

1. Pray that God will speak to you. Quieten yourself and let go of whatever distractions may be occupying your mind at the time; just let them fade into the background for the next 30-60 minutes.

Just put them all into God's hands and ask him to help you to hear him speaking, and to focus on his words.

2. Read the section of Mark (I have used the Good News version of the Bible, but you can use whatever version you're comfortable with). Resist the temptation to peek at the notes or even the headings. But you might like to read just the little introduction paragraph at the top, to get you going. Once you have read the section of Mark, go back and underline the parts that spoke out to you most strongly, thinking about why it stood out. Then circle the words or phrases you don't understand or find most puzzling. Think and pray for a minute, looking for some answers. Write down your questions and what you think might be some possible answers.
3. Now go through the question sheet. These questions are designed to cover a range of things that come from the passage. Some may be more relevant for you, so concentrate on them rather than feeling you have to answer them all (this isn't a school test, but just a tool to get you thinking about Jesus!). Hopefully you will come to study group with lots of wonderful insights and questions to share! And even if you don't get to do these questions at all, as part of preparation for study group, don't let that stop you from going to study group; we all learn differently; we all have different weekly pressures and study capabilities. Feel free to rock up without any preparation at all if necessary, because there will be lots of things to share anyway, even if this is the first time you read the passage.
4. Now read through my notes.
5. Pray again, keeping in mind the one or two strongest things that God has said to you. Talk to God about these things, whether it be to thank him, or hand something over to him, or to ask him for something. He knows you, he loves you, he hears you, and he

wants to bless you powerfully through his Son Jesus, our Saviour and Lord.

6. If you have any nagging questions afterwards, go and ask a reliable, Bible-based pastor, and be patient. (If all else fails, you can contact me at the locations listed on the back of this book). Don't expect all your questions to be answered straight away from just one or two Bible studies. Allow time for the *whole* story to inform you.

May God bless you richly, as he speaks to you from his word.

Time For Acknowledgement

'Who is Jesus?'

Read **Mark 1: 1 - 13**

There are 4 Gospels, which give an account of the life, death and resurrection of Jesus: Matthew, Mark, Luke and John. Mark is very different from the others because it is the shortest. Mark doesn't say anything about the first 30 years of Jesus' life, but jumps straight in at the point when Jesus began his special work. Mark is a straightforward Gospel that gets right into the action of what Jesus did and said. He is very excited about telling people who Jesus is, and how he is Good News – the best news - for all the world. He wants us to get to know Jesus, because Jesus can completely change our lives.

Questions: Why do you think Mark doesn't tell us about where Jesus came from, as John, Luke and Matthew do?

The quote from Isaiah contains the image of clearing or straightening a **road**. What were the roads like in those days? How much work would it take to smooth or straighten a road? What sort of person would people go to so much trouble for?

If John is encouraging the people to 'prepare the way' for Jesus, the king of the universe, how are they supposed to 'clear the road' (i.e. in spiritual terms)?

Why would ***Jesus*** need to be baptized, since we know from elsewhere in the New Testament that he was without sin?

If Jesus needed the Holy Spirit to accomplish his mission, to do what God wanted for him, then how much more do ***we*** need the Holy Spirit?

1. John the Baptist (verses 1-8)

John the Baptist is very important to all the gospel writers, because John points to the meaning of Jesus. Jesus didn't come into history from nowhere - there is a long history about him before he even arrives, and that history is found in the Old Testament - all 4,000 years of it! All of this preparation is building up to Jesus, pointing forward to Jesus. What happens in the Old Testament has a pattern: God blesses people; people enjoy peace for a short time; people start taking God for granted, and they turn away from God and fall into sin (doing things their own way); God calls them back but they continue to sin; God judges them and punishes them; then people turn back to God; and God blesses them again. Over and over again this happens. The problem of course, which is never overcome in the Old Testament, is sin. God wants to bless people, but they keep falling into sin. John works out in 'the wilderness', which is where Israel often ended up, wandering around in sin.

What John the Baptist does is he sums up the message of the Old Testament, by telling people to repent, to ***turn away from their sin*** and ***turn back to God*** - like doing a U-turn (v.4). He is a prophet sent by God, and this is what prophets do. But more than that, he is preparing people for Jesus to come. And the Old Testament speaks about this John, as Mark points out from the book of Isaiah "I will send my messenger ahead of you... Get the road ready for the Lord"(v.2-3). So John is saying 'Get ready! The King we have all been waiting for is coming! The one who will take away our sins and give us peace and blessing from God!' This is what he means in verse 7, when he talks about someone much greater than him who was coming - someone who would baptize with the Holy Spirit. What is happening here is absolutely huge - the biggest event in all of history - ***God's own Son coming to save the world.*** Think of it this way: John and Jesus stand like the two sides of a hinge - the centre hinge of all history - John is the last prophet of the Old Testament and Jesus opens up the New Testament, which involves something completely new - the forgiveness of sins for all the world.

How do we come to know Jesus? In the same way that John was indicating - by repenting. This means to turn away from our sins, the things that mess up our lives and make us feel so bad about ourselves. We need to be honest with ourselves and not hide from the truth about our sin. But we also need to turn to God, be honest with God, because now that Jesus has come, God will forgive our sins and give us his Holy Spirit - which means a whole new life for us. This is "Good News" indeed, about God's own Son coming, as Mark says in verse 1. Do you want to know this Jesus? then repent of your old life, turn away from it, and turn to God. Ask God to send his Holy Spirit into your life, to bring understanding and new life. This is what happens when we read God's word -the Bible- with an open heart and mind; God speaks to us, revealing the truth.

2. Jesus is Baptized (verses 9-13)

John the Baptist makes the people walk into the river and he 'dunks' them. This is a sign that the person has truly repented, that they are 'cleaning up' their old life of sin, to start a fresh, new life. So why does ***Jesus*** get baptized? He hasn't sinned, he doesn't need to turn away from a bad old life. Well there are 3 powerful things happening when Jesus gets baptized:

1) Jesus is doing this in obedience to God his Father, so that Jesus gets even closer to regular people. Ritual cleansing was something Jewish people always did when preparing to go to a religious feast and special occasions, to 'wash away' their sins. Even though Jesus is God's son, and he doesn't sin, he submits to this terrible thing really, washing himself in the same dirty water all these sinners have. It's as if, by going down into the water, he's not washing anything off, but taking something on - our sins. This is an act which declares he is taking our sins on his shoulders, in order to die for them, to take them to the cross and deal with them. This is an act of obedience to his Father, because this was why he was sent, to die for our sins. And so when he submits to being baptized, his Father speaks the words of approval from Heaven "You are my own dear Son. I am pleased with you"(v.11). From beginning to end, Jesus' mission is to deal with ***our*** sins. See how much he loves us, to do such a thing so willingly!

   Do you think the world doesn't need this? Have a look around. We see our world spiraling down into greater and greater destruction, depression, corruption and self-interest. What the world needs now is Jesus in our lives.

2) Jesus, like the great King David in the Old Testament, receives the Holy Spirit to help him in his mission. Jesus is truly human and is really tempted to sin like any other person. This time spent being tempted in 'the wilderness' was significant. But he has a Helper, and he has the power of God in the Holy Spirit to do the miraculous things he will do. Jesus must co-operate with this Holy Spirit, for him to resist sin, and to trust God's Spirit to work powerfully when he prays and commands miracles to happen. Again, he is truly human, and he must trust in God the same as we do. Now if Jesus needed the Holy Spirit to help him, what about us? Lots of people think they can get their lives right by doing things in their own strength. But that is just foolish. We need to depend on God, and have his Spirit come into our lives to change our lives. Pray that the Holy Spirit will come into your life and work powerfully to change you.
3) When Jesus receives the Holy Spirit like this, God's great plan for the world is just about ready to explode, like the bud of a flower ready to bloom. Through Jesus' work and death on the cross, the Holy Spirit will be poured out on many, many people. This too was promised in the Old Testament (Joel 2:28-29). Jesus is like God's 'funnel', where God pours his Spirit through Jesus, out onto millions. This special presence of God, living in us, so that we really know God in our hearts and lives, this can only come through ***Jesus***. His death and resurrection break the power of death and sin, and pour out God's blessing like never before. This is the most spectacular and important event in the history of the universe. Let's praise God, and thank him for this wonderful gift he has given us through his Son Jesus!

Special note: Repent is the original word, translated here "turn away from your sins", but this is only half of the meaning, the second half being "turn back to God"

Reflect and pray: How important are repentance and the presence of the Holy Spirit in your life? There are so many things we simply cannot change by ourselves, like the effects of abuse, our many mistakes in life, the bad habits we've inherited from our family. These things can weigh us down, or we can ignore them with arrogance and pride. But the damage remains and affects us to the point of being damaging to others. Only God can really deal with these things in a permanent way that renews us in the present and way off in the future. Speak openly and honestly to God, expecting to meet the real and powerful Jesus Christ.

'Jesus takes over'

Read **Mark 1: 14 - 28**

The preparation for Jesus' work has been done, (and John the Baptist continues to do that for some time) but now Jesus takes over more and more each day. And what a powerful start he makes! 2 things stand out - his ***message*** and his ***authority***. Jesus comes with the authority of God. He is God's King. God's Spirit is working in him with real power to speak and to act, because the "Kingdom of God" is breaking into the world (v.15). This is God himself coming, as promised in the Old Testament - God coming to rule over people's lives with goodness and power like never before. So Jesus starts to ***take*** people and ***teach*** people, and ***free*** people from the rule of Satan and his demons.

Questions: Is there something similar about Jesus' message (v.15) and John's from last week (v.4)? And what is ***different*** about their message?

What does Jesus mean when he says, "The ***Kingdom of God*** is near"?

Why do you think the 4 fishermen followed Jesus?

What do you think it means when Mark says Jesus "taught with ***authority***"(v.22)?

How can the casting out of the demon be considered a "new ***teaching***"(v.27)?

Why do you think Jesus called lowly fishermen to be his leading disciples?

1. Jesus' message (v.14-15)

John was put into prison for his message of repentance. Notice how Jesus' ***message*** is very similar to John's, also saying "Turn away from your sins" (v.15). But instead of adding "and be baptized", like John did, Jesus adds "and believe the Good News!" Something very big has changed, when Jesus starts his work. Through Jesus, the great time of God's blessing is starting, and this is "Good News"(which is the same word as "Gospel"). So Jesus went to Galilee and "preached the ***Good News*** from God"(v.14). Now Jesus, like John, wants people to start by turning away from their sins, their old life, and turn to God to hear this Gospel, this good news. This message is coming ***from God*** - God is offering a whole new life through Jesus. As John the Baptist said, this Jesus will wash people with the Holy Spirit, giving them a whole new life, a new start with God and power to change from the old bad life. We need to hear and ***believe*** this message, because it's through accepting the good ***news*** in our hearts that we receive the good ***things*** of life and love and power that Jesus brings. This is God's message to all people, and it's a message that changes lives, bringing the Kingdom of God to rule in our lives.

2. Jesus' authority (v.16-28)

Very quickly we see Jesus gathering people around him. He chooses people, and calls them to leave everything behind and follow him, to be his disciples (which means 'learners' or 'students'). These disciples will travel with Jesus and learn closely about what he is doing. Notice how Jesus calls these men and "at once" they follow him. They see and hear a man with special authority, so that when he calls, they go. Even James and John, who leave their father in the boat "with the hired men" - this means their father owns a fishing ***business*** - his sons walk off. These men are an example for us - when Jesus calls them, they leave their old life behind, to follow him. These 4 men are leaving their careers catching fish, to start 'catching people' for God's Kingdom.

What sort of things is God calling ***you*** to leave behind? A life of lying and cheating? Anger and resentment? Loving money or lusting after sex? It could be any of these or many more. These things leave us empty and sad. Well Jesus says in effect 'Give it up! Leave it behind! And take on the new life I have to offer! - follow me.'

There are then 2 more ways Jesus shows his authority - in the way he teaches and the way he casts out demons. The people "***were amazed*** at the way he taught, for he wasn't like the teachers of the Law; instead, he taught ***with authority***"(v.22) and "What is this?...This man ***has authority*** to give orders to the evil spirits, and they obey him!"(v.27). When Jesus speaks, people and demons listen. It's not just that he is a good speaker, but that he is speaking with the authority of ***God***. People clearly hear the power of God in what he says. And he is not looking to other people for his authority. Jesus wouldn't say "***Rabbi*** such-and-such says this, so we should do it", or he doesn't say to the demons "In the name of ***Moses*** I cast you out". No, Jesus says things like "***I*** tell you.... ***I*** cast you out, demon!"(see Matthew 5: 21-37, & Mark 5: 1-20). Jesus comes with the authority to speak directly from God. So what does this mean to us? It means we can be sure this is ***the*** Son of God, who comes ***from*** God. The demons know this (v.24). This is no ordinary man, but God's own Son, God's King, coming with all the authority of God's Kingdom.

3. The People Jesus Chooses

One more important thing to notice is the sort of people Jesus chooses to follow him. He doesn't choose earthly kings or princes, or greatly educated people, or even religious leaders. He chooses ***ordinary*** people. His first 4 disciples are just fishermen. One of the clear proofs about God's message and power in Jesus is what God does with these people and others - both men and women - after Jesus' death and resurrection. Their lives will be radically changed. They will go from being lowly fishermen to being powerful preachers who perform the same miracles Jesus does. And even slow, stupid Simon (Later renamed Peter), who keeps getting everything wrong as we read later in Mark, this Simon/Peter will later write one of the greatest letters in the New Testament. This is very encouraging for us, because no matter who we are, or how ***low*** a person we might think we are, Jesus is calling ***us***. Of course there will also be rich people he calls, like Matthew, and educated people like Luke, and influential people like Paul. But he starts with the lowly, ordinary people, to show that no-one is excluded. No-one is too bad, or too boring, or too dumb to come into the

Kingdom of God, because God loves us all equally. This message is powerful to change anyone.

So what about you? - "Repent and believe the Good News!" Follow the Son of God who comes with all the authority of God, to give you a whole new life.

Reflect and pray: How much are you following Jesus with all your life, submitting to his authority rather than all those other things and people that seek to have power over us? No matter how small you may feel, you have great purpose in God's plan. Pray to see things the way God does, about you and the world around you, to see the truth about Jesus and his mission to set us free. I promise you, when the lights go on, your life will be changed forever, filled with the love of God that can never be taken away from you.

'Hidden Power'

Read **Mark 1: 29 45**

It's very clear from the first 2 parts of chapter 1 that this man Jesus, the King from Heaven, had great power and authority. He could have taken over all of Judea and the surrounding area if he wanted to. But this was not the way God wanted him to be King. If he was going to succeed in his mission, it would be by the power of his love. In this section we see his compassion and care for people. We see him starting work before daylight and working well into the night healing people, preaching and casting out demons. But if he was going to succeed in his mission, he also had to stay 'under cover', not drawing too much attention from the authorities. It was vitally important for Jesus to get in 3 years of ministry, working with people, before he headed for the cross. He had a great deal to teach, so that his disciples and others really understood what was going on. If he died too soon, the true message of the Good News might have become lost or twisted into something false, after he went back to Heaven.

Questions: How would Simon's mother-in-law have felt, when a notable, important person like Jesus visits, and she can't get out of bed to offer hospitality? (especially in those days)

How long a working day did Jesus have? Why?

What is the common element in these 3 stories, that shows us something of Jesus' attitude to people?

Why would Jesus send the man to the temple to offer a sacrifice?

Why did Jesus tell the demons and the man to keep quiet?

Why do you think, the man ignored this? Would we judge him as being disobedient, or is he meant to be a good example for us?

1. Jesus' Love (v.29-34)

It always puts a cheeky smile on my face when I read this story. You know that Jesus really loves *everybody,* when you see him even healing mothers-in-law! Either that, or Jesus has a good sense of humour and wants Simon to suffer a bit, making him love his mother-in-law. (I can imagine Simon holding his head in his hands thinking "Now what did he go and do **that** for? I had her just where I wanted her!"). But jokes aside, there is something wonderful happening here in this story and the next one with the man.

Jesus loves people, and he loves them to be functioning well. Notice how "*as soon as Jesus arrived,* he was told about her and *went to her (v.* 30-31) and in the 2nd story Jesus *was filled with pity" (v.41).* He **loves** them both and heals them straight away. But this means they can *now function well.* They can resume their place in the community; they can do again what is important for them to be doing. They want to be useful and play their part in family and community as regular people. To God, everyone is valuable, and has an important part to play in the community. Jesus loves these two enough to restore their self respect and get them 'back in circulation' with their friends, family and workmates.

Simon's mother-in-law is obviously in charge of the household, and takes pride in being the host when friends drop in. So, Jesus "took her by the hand and helped her up. The fever left her, and ***she began to wait on them."*** This is her valuable role within the family, and she would have been ***very*** upset for Jesus to visit when she was not able to show hospitality. The man with the skin disease also has been cut off from his role in society. He had to keep his distance from everybody, unable to work and not allowed to take his place in worshipping God with the rest of his community in the synagogue and the temple. So once Jesus heals him, he "sent him away at once" to go to the priest and "offer the sacrifice that Moses ordered" as a sign of his thanks to God and his reentry into the community. Jesus loves him, and wants him to take up his proper place again.

Jesus' love is so strong and so pure. He doesn't just say "I love you" and give people a pat on the back and then leave. He really loves them and he's keen to see them functioning well again. Most of all, he wants them to experience the joy of serving God, taking their place among the people of God. When Simon's motherinlaw "began to wait on them" she was serving God, she was serving Jesus. When the man went to the synagogue to offer the sacrifice, he was serving God, giving thanks to God. This is the proper place for all of us; God may have different ways for each of us to serve him, but all of us have a job to do there are no 'passengers'

What about you? What sorts of things are you suffering from that stop you from serving God and functioning well in your community? Do you know that Jesus can heal you? Do you know that Jesus thinks you're valuable and you have an important role to play? With Jesus by our side, we can love people the way he does, and contribute to the building up of people around us in our family, with our friends, and at work. What a great job God gives us to do! It's what we do that benefits others in substantial, significant ways, that really matters in life. Not the cars, the house, the job, the lavish holidays, but the people.

2. Jesus Keeps Moving (v.35-39)

Jesus is so concerned about teaching and healing people. He wants to touch as many lives as possible. He works from dawn to dusk, and he doesn't just sit in one place and spend all his time relaxing with his closest friends. He says "We must go on to the other villages around here. I have come to preach in them also, because that is why I came" (v.38). God's concern for people is for *all* people. Jesus' job is to spread the Good News as far as he can, and this is something we need to learn too. When we find our place in the people of God, we have a role to play in spreading the Good News about Jesus. If this was his first priority, then it's ours too, because Jesus died for *all* people, not just us. Our new place in God's Kingdom is not something for us to selfishly hold onto. Rather, if Jesus' love has come into our hearts, then we should be fired up with concern for people like he was not just by helping with practical things, but by giving the message about Jesus' love too, so that these people can have a whole new life also. God has given each of us gifts to use in serving others find what your gifts are, even if they're plain gifts like Simon's mother-in-law had. But then God also gives us **voices** to praise him in what we do voices to speak to God (notice how Jesus spends time ***praying*** before he makes a move) and voices to speak to others, in praise of God. Have you shown somebody some love lately the pure love that comes from Jesus, using your gifts? And have you ***spoken*** to that person about your reason for loving them Jesus' love in **your life?** Try it, and see the powerful things God might do.

3. The Word Gets Out (v.43)

Twice in these stories Jesus tells people to keep quiet about him (v.34 to demons, and v.44 to the man). As I explained above, this was so Jesus would not attract too much attention too quickly. But look at what the man does in verse 45. He is just so excited that he ***can't*** contain himself. This Good News is so powerful to change people's lives that not even Jesus could keep a lid on it. And so again for us, if this powerful Word has changed our lives, and we are as thankful to God as this man was, then how can we keep quiet about it? If the Good News about Jesus has really changed us, then it gives us power to change, but also power to witness boldly with our friends, family and workmates.

Reflect and pray for God's love to come into your life, as the Apostle Paul says in Romans 5:5, "God's love has been poured into our hearts through the Holy Spirit."

'The Greatest Healer'

Read **Mark 2: 1 – 12**

This story about Jesus healing the paralysed man is the first of the really tense 'high points' in Mark's Gospel. When Jesus says in verse 10 "the Son of Man has authority on earth to forgive sins," everyone around him must have stopped breathing from shock. Many would have been ready to stone him to death, because he was saying things that only God had the right to say. This story again focuses on Jesus' **authority,** like in the middle of chapter one. What comes between that event and this story is a focus on Jesus' love and concern for people to be whole and functioning well again. Now we see these two themes coming together: Jesus has the ultimate authority to forgive sins, and what he is doing with this man is making the ***whole man*** well again inside and out. Jesus loves and cares for the whole person. He is the greatest healer. He came to heal our minds and hearts and consciences, not just our bodies. And he could only do that by bringing forgiveness for our sins, to make our souls healthy and pure again. This is the real aim of his whole life to die on the cross to forgive our sins. This is the most powerful healing a person can ever experience.

Questions: Why do you think Jesus say what he said in verse 5?

Do you think Jesus only cares about the man's **physical** ailment?

Which do you think is more important his physical or spiritual healing? Which do you think is more important for us? Why?

How does Jesus' healing of the man's paralysis **prove** that he has authority to forgive sins? Which is easier, to say, 'your sins are forgiven' or 'Get up, pick up your mat, and walk'? Why?

Whose faith prompted Jesus to act? (v.5) What does this say to people who protest, "My faith is a private thing, just between me and God"?

1. Jesus Heals the Whole Man

It's a strange thing, isn't it, when this paralysed man is brought to Jesus for healing and the first thing Jesus says is "My son, your sins are forgiven." Jesus sees what is happening inside this man's life, and he addresses that first. Jesus must have had a reason to say this; I don't think he would say it just to provoke the Pharisees. There must have been some sin that had this man really worried. Either that, or the man ***thought that*** his sins had brought on his illness as God's punishment on him. Whatever the case, Jesus is dealing with the man's deepest need first, to know that God can heal him inside by forgiving his sins, to know that God **wants** to forgive his sins and can forgive his sins through Jesus. When Jesus asks the question "Is it easier to say, 'Your sins are forgiven' or "Get up, pick up your mat and walk'? " the answer is that the first statement is easier. Anyone could say that and there would be no way to prove it. But Jesus can prove his authority to forgive sins, by going on to heal the man. How does this prove anything? Because only God can give Jesus power to heal such an illness, and if Jesus is lying about his authority to forgive sins then God would not honour Jesus by giving him power to heal the man. The healing is God's sign that what Jesus says here is true Jesus really can forgive people's sins.

This story is here to encourage us to *believe in* Jesus he has great power and authority to give us a whole new life.

But there is something else happening here. The teachers of the law who "were sitting there" would have certainly thought his disability was caused by his sin. "He is being judged by God for what he has done" is what they would be thinking. Now that sort of thing can happen sometimes, because God is powerful and free to do that if he wants to. Very often it would work like this: This man might have been a robber, who had robbed a house by climbing through the roof. As he was escaping with the loot, he might have slipped on the roof, fallen to the ground and ended up a quadriplegic, paralysed from the neck down. People would say he got what he deserved; God let him be paralysed as part of God's judgement on his sin. This may in fact be what happened, who knows? We're not told. But it could also be that this man ended up paralysed through no fault of his own. He may have even been born that way. We're not told the details because it doesn't matter. The Jewish leaders would have been thinking "there's no way God will heal this man, because it's a sign of his sin", but to Jesus it **doesn't matter** how big or bad a person's sin is, God can forgive through him. All that matters to Jesus is a person wanting to come to him and be forgiven, to be healed on the inside and be given new hope and a new life. Not just to be thinking about things that affect the outside of our bodies, like being able to walk, but things that affect our soul, our relationship with God. Notice how Jesus forgives the man's sins first, while he is still paralysed.

When Jesus said to this man "Your sins are forgiven" the man could have said "No thank you, I just came to have my body healed." That's the way lots of people think today. They only care about what they see, and they don't really want their inside yucky lives to be healed and made pure. This would make a person only half healed, and that's not the way Jesus works. He cares about the whole person. And if you think you can pick and choose with Jesus, you're wrong. If you don't want the inside healing Jesus can give, you may as well stay sick with all your physical illnesses, because you'll never be really happy and well anyway. Be like this man; accept the complete healing he offers you.

2. Faith is Involved

The friends of this man, who carried him to the roof and let him down on the stretcher just to get close, showed great faith. Mark says, "Seeing how much faith *they* had, Jesus said..." This is the first time the word "faith" or "believe" (the same word) has been used in Mark since 1: 14 where Jesus says, "Repent and *believe the* Good News". It's when people show faith in God that things really happen. This is the whole point of the Bible, that if people only trusted God and followed his ways we would all be greatly blessed and a whole lot happier. These friends of the man obviously trust in Jesus' ability to heal. For them, there is no question about his authority and power, they simply believe, because they have heard the Good News about him. God had promised to send the Messiah, God's great King, and they just simply trusted that here it was happening. They believed because they knew God could be trusted, from all the stories they had read in the Old Testament. And they were acting like God does, by bringing their friend on the stretcher. Many times in the past God had "carried his people" when they were injured and tired and sick. These friends weren't thinking of themselves but thinking of God and their friend. They are a great example of faith, and how faith is not something we just do alone. Jesus isn't inspired to heal this man because of his faith, but his friends' faith.

Very often we think of our faith as a private thing that has nothing to do with anyone else but that's not true. If God has blessed us and we believe in him, then we can't just greedily keep it to ourselves. If we are filled with

God's love for other people, then we should be inspired to do crazy things to encourage our friends in faith, like these men did with their friend. Who knows this man might not have even wanted to come to Jesus for healing. But his friends might have said "We know you, Fred. You're in great suffering and we love you. If you just trust in this Jesus, God will bless you. Even if you don't want to go, we're taking you anyway." When Jesus forgave this man's sins, and then healed him, he would be in no doubt at all that his friends' faith was faith in the true and powerful God. He would value those friends even more, because they had the courage to show so much faith in God out of their love for him.

If you're a Christian, then don't be a 'private' one. If you really love your friends and family then be **a faithful** Christian and serve them **in Jesus' name.** If you're not a Christian, but have Christian friends around you, then realise the greatest thing they can do to love you is talking to you about their faith in Jesus, "bringing you to Jesus" like the friends did with the man, and encouraging you to see His great love for you.

Reflect and pray about those things in your life, where you need forgiveness and healing. Ask God to help, because sometimes it can take time for healing to happen. Ask God to bring loving brothers and sisters into your life to encourage and help you along the way. Ask God to save you from the shallowness that only seeks physical, outward healing. Ask him to speak clearly into the deeper parts of your life.

CHAPTER 2

Time for Change

'Jesus is Lord, so things must change'

Read **Mark 2: 13-28**

There are three very different incidents which happen one after another in this section of Mark. They are different incidents, but there is a common message: ***When Jesus comes into a person's life, things must change, not just stay the same.***

Jesus is not just someone who comes to make people feel better, to be a "Doctor Feelgood" who understands them, loves them, gives them a pat on the head and promises to come back next week for another dose of encouragement. Of course Jesus does understand us, love us, encourage us, and promises to be there for those who believe in him, but there is much more to Jesus than just that. Jesus also calls people to ***follow*** him, he challenges people to change their way of ***thinking***, and their way of ***doing things***. If you only accept half (the easy half) of what Jesus offers you, you only accept a small Jesus; you keep him small, like a good-luck charm sitting on a mantlepiece. This does not honour Jesus, but dishonours him. This does not please God, but makes him angry. This does not give a person security, but quite the opposite. People often think they can use God in their own small way, but God is not like that. Jesus is not just our buddy when we need a shoulder to cry on, he is our LORD. He wants us to be loyal to him, devoted to him because he loves us. He wants your whole life to be changed, with new purpose, with power over those things that seek to drag you down. Jesus wants to give us a special dignity and honour, to become God's loved children, a prince or princess in the service of our great King.

Questions: Why do you think Jesus would choose a person like Levi?

How do you think Levi's lifestyle might have changed after meeting Jesus?

How should we treat people regarded as 'lowly sinners' in our church?

What does the reaction of the Pharisees say about their attitude of heart?

Is Levi an example for all Christians? How?

What do the latter two sections here have in common with the first one?

How important is Jesus' presence for the Jewish religion?

When is "the bridegroom taken away from them"?

How hard is it to change habits you have had for many years? What can you do about it?

1. Jesus Calls a Tax-collector v.13-17

This first story shows us very clearly how Jesus is not out to play favourites. Jesus doesn't choose all the highly respected 'religious' people to be his disciples, he calls ordinary people – fishermen and even tax-collectors. Tax-collectors in particular were regarded as 'scum' by the Jews, because they were taking money from God's people and giving it to the Roman authorities. (The Roman Empire had taken control of Israel and all the land around it many years before). Tax collectors were traitors, and not only that, but they would also charge too much tax, in order to put extra money in their own pockets and become rich.

So you can understand the reaction of shock and horror in verse 16, when Jesus publicly chooses one of these people to follow him. We are even told that "A large number of tax-collectors and other outcasts were following Jesus." (verse 15). It should be a great comfort to us to know that Jesus accepts ***anyone*** – no matter what background we come from or what we have done in our past. Other people might look down on us for what we are, but Jesus looks at ***who we are*** and ***what we can become*** with his help. Jesus answers these people by in effect saying "Sure, these tax-collectors are obviously sinners, but that is why I came, to ***save sinners***! If you think you're too good, not a sinner, then okay, you ***won't*** be saved, you won't be healed of all the rotten things in your life." All of us need to think carefully about these 2 possible responses to Jesus – 1) we can be like the people standing by who think they don't need Jesus. This is being dishonest with God, because we have all sinned and need God's powerful healing in our lives. Or 2) we can be like this tax-collector and follow Jesus when he calls us. We can be honest with God and ourselves, and confess openly that we have sinned. In this way we will be healed and know a whole new life.

But then there is something more – we don't just do this in our heads. Jesus calls Levi to ***actually follow*** him – to get off his backside, leave his old rotten life behind, and join this rag-tag bunch of sinners who want to ***learn*** from Jesus and ***grow*** together. Notice how Jesus comes to Levi (whose other name is Matthew, in Matthew's Gospel)- Jesus goes out of his way to show his love for this man who other people hated. This is a great thing for us to appreciate; just how much Jesus loves us and will meet us where we are. But then Jesus commands Levi to follow him. Jesus isn't going to just 'drop in' each week to be his counsellor, to make him feel good. And Levi doesn't answer Jesus with "Can I make an appointment for next Monday?" No, Jesus expects him to respond to his challenge, to play his part in this new relationship and follow Jesus. Jesus hasn't met Levi just to leave him where he is. Jesus loves him enough to want him to move on, to help him in a big way. Jesus wants Levi's life to be totally changed, with all the power God has to offer him, through Jesus.

It's exactly the same for us – God often wants more for us than we even realize, but we'll never know until we say "Yes" to him, and that means to follow him all the way. If you are feeling that you haven't really said this to God, then do it now. Pray earnestly and honestly, confessing all your sins and turning away from your old life. Put yourself into His hands, and commit yourself to following this great loving Lord.

But also don't despise the church God has given you to help as well. Levi didn't follow Jesus alone; he joined a group. And Levi didn't choose who were in that group, Jesus did. The church is where you can be encouraged and where God has provided teachers and pastors and an opportunity for you to learn more about Jesus. And remember – don't look down on the other sinners God has chosen, like the 'religious' people around Jesus did.

2. Other pictures of change v.18-28

These other two incidents, where the Pharisees challenge Jesus about fasting and picking wheat on the Sabbath, show us the same point that has been made with Levi – now Jesus is here, things change. Since Jesus, the wonderful Saviour from God has come, it is an exciting time for great celebration, not a time to fast. People should be bursting with joy. But now also the old religion has to accommodate the new changes Jesus brings – this is the meaning of the "new wine in old wineskins "picture. This is all about making the appropriate response to Jesus – our response should be one of joy and acceptance, not sadness and bitterness like the Pharisees are doing.

The same goes for the law about the Sabbath. Jesus corrects a bad understanding; the sabbath is not supposed to be a burden but a joy – picking a few grains when you're hungry surely doesn't qualify as 'work', like the Pharisees had classed it. They were so caught up in doing everything right by the Law that it created a blockage of pride, instead of an openness and humility which recognizes that Jesus meets their real need. No wonder Jesus never chose a Pharisee to be one of his disciples; it's a case of, "O Lord, it's hard to be humble, when you're perfect in every way." Instead, they should have given up their legalism, and seen their LORD who had come among them, to change them deeply inside, and fill them with joy, rest, peace, and everything else God had promised would come.

What is ***your*** response to Jesus?

Reflect and pray about the things God might want to change in your life. No matter how difficult that might seem, ask the Lord to be with you in the process of transforming your life, and He will. Ask him to also give you a heart of grace towards the others in God's church around you, because none of us are perfect.

'The Battle Lines are Drawn'

Read **Mark 3: 1 – 19**

At the end of chapter 2 we saw how different groups came to Jesus asking him about the strange things he was doing. "Why does he eat with outcasts? ... Why don't your disciples fast?... Why do you pick wheat on the Sabbath?" These were fairly polite, reasonable questions. But before long, here in chapter 3, they become nasty and menacing. The questions from the authorities are designed to trap and accuse Jesus, planning to kill him. The 3 parts of verses 1-19 all highlight the fact that a battle has begun. The battle lines are drawn between Jesus and the Jewish authorities, between Jesus and the evil spirits, and also between Jesus' disciples and the evil spirits. There is a war going on – a spiritual war.

Questions: Why does Jesus heal this man on the sabbath? Why doesn't he make an appointment for the next day?

Why are the Pharisees so violently opposed to him?

Is Jesus throwing out the Law altogether? Does God 'work' on the sabbath?

How would you describe Jesus' attitude & relationship to the Pharisees? What about the evil spirits (v.11)?

What is the significance of Jesus choosing ***12*** Apostles? Why does he plan to send them out to preach & cast out demons (as he will do in ch.6)?

What do you think is the common theme in these 3 stories?

1. Jesus versus the Authorities. (v.1-6)

The Jewish authorities are clearly on the wrong side in this spiritual war. They have unwittingly sided with Satan in 2 ways: by plotting Jesus' death, and by taking the laws God gave and twisting them out of shape. The first thing to notice is that Jesus himself is a good Jew. He respects God's words in the Bible, and the commandment God gave about keeping the Sabbath holy, by not working, but resting and worshipping God. So here is Jesus one Saturday, taking a day off – not teaching the crowds or travelling from town to town. He's worshipping God in the synagogue. But Jesus knew he was being watched. He had been criticized for picking wheat on the Sabbath in chapter 2, and now he could see there was another example of the same misunderstanding right here in the synagogue. He could teach a very important lesson to correct that misunderstanding, by healing this man on the Sabbath.

You see, the Jews had become so obsessed with getting everything perfect in their obedience to God's law, that they were now missing the point of it all. The law was not meant to weigh people down and oppress them, it was meant to improve their life and give them peace, safety and happiness, like our civil laws today are meant to. The Sabbath law was a very good thing, designed to give people a day of rest, instead of working themselves to death 7 days a week. But if someone urgently needed help, and someone else could provide that help, (which means work), then this is more important. The Sabbath is a sign of God's love for his people, and it's supposed to encourage them to ***love*** each other better, not ***stop*** loving on the Sabbath.

Notice that what Jesus does to heal this man is very simple, with little effort. He says a few words; it's not like he spent half the day rebuilding his house. Also note that Jesus ***could*** maybe have caught up with this man on the next day if he really wanted to. But once people were crowded around when he starts work, things get pretty hectic. Right here and now might in fact be the only opportunity he'll have to show this man God's power and love. And why shouldn't that happen on a Sabbath, (after all, he ***is God***, and can heal on the sabbath if he wants to) and do it in a way that points clearly to who he is, so this man will believe in him? This is the big point to keep in mind with all these miracles – they are something ***more important than just healing people*** – people need to ***believe*** in Jesus. Do ***you*** truly believe in Jesus? The miracles are pointers to show us who Jesus is – The Messiah, the Son of God, who is sent to make things right. People need to believe in him – even this paralyzed man, so that when Jesus dies on the cross their sins will be forgiven and a new relationship with God will begin. This miracle with the man's hand is chickenfeed compared to the main event, the miracle on the cross.

But just as many people will believe in Jesus, there will also be great opposition to him. The forces of evil don't want him to succeed, and they react violently to such good things happening (and it's the same today). The Pharisees are unknowingly working for Satan, not God, because they have given in to greed and hunger for power, wanting control over people instead of serving them. They have given into temptation and so they have a distorted view of what they are doing and saying. On the surface they think they are doing right when in fact if they searched their hearts they would know they are being downright evil. And so they make plans to kill Jesus.

2. Jesus versus the Evil Spirits (v.7-12)

The Pharisees are a visible sign of the evil opposition to Jesus. But there is another group, an ***in***visible group, who are behind all this. And Jesus is able to expose them when they interfere in a helpless victim's life. Jesus can cast out a demon from someone who doesn't want that demon around. With the Pharisees, however, it's different, because they have willingly given into the ways of evil, and don't want to part with it. The evil spirits straight away recognize who Jesus is (v.11). But Jesus doesn't want them 'blowing his cover' too soon (v.12); that might have led to him being killed before he had enough time to teach people. Jesus needs time to spend with his disciples, building up their faith and understanding about him and what God was doing. His miracles need teaching to go with them, and Mark has been making this point (see 1:14,21,27,38; 2:2,13). As always, clear teaching is the best weapon against the confusion and chaos that Satan works in people's lives. And for Jesus it was important not to leave behind a cloud of uncertainty after his death, so he tells the spirits to be quiet. For the masses of people who didn't understand what was going on at this point, all these miracles would at least show God was working. God was declaring war on the forces of evil, in a decisive and permanent way. This should be a great encouragement to us, because it's all the evil things in life that drag us down and hurt us, and God has acted in a big way to fight for us – and win.

3. The Disciples Versus the Evil Spirits (v.13-19)

To show how much this was ***God's*** work, and God's great time of change, Jesus not only fights this battle himself, but he is going to send out a 'battalion', the first 12 disciples he had chosen. These 12 represent the 12 tribes of Israel which God had created thousands of years before. In choosing 12 and sending them out, it was meant to show that he was 'remaking' the people of God, and giving them power to go out and battle in a new way, a more powerful way than ever before. They were to meet the forces of evil directly, and bring people to the truth (by preaching v.14), instead of the old way of fighting, where you kill the enemy. This is the most powerful thing in the world, to change a human life and free them from evil.

This is very helpful for us. We need to appreciate that there is a spiritual battle going on today. And Jesus, through his Holy Spirit, can give us everything we need to fight this battle: understanding; love for other people; eyes to see when something is truly good or evil; faith and strength not to give into evil like the Pharisees did, but joyfully follow God; and also the power to overcome the evil things that affect us. This is the great battle of love over evil, which we are supposed to engage in, not run away from, knowing that God is fighting for us. These events in chapter 3 point forward to the 'main event' where the big battle is won by Jesus, on the cross. After that victory, God's people have power to win over evil and fight in the battle like never before. And what's more, one day Jesus will return to bring this war to an end, swiftly and easily (see Revelation 12:1-12 & 20:1-10).

'The Empire Strikes Back'

Read **Mark 3: 20 – 35**

In the previous section Jesus has declared war on the evil spiritual world, a world that operates through leaders who twist God's truth and plan to kill Jesus (3:1-6). It also works through evil spirits who dominate people's lives (3:7-12). This battle against evil was not just Jesus acting, but God, who was building a new people (3:13-19). In 3:20-35 Satan's vicious counter-attack comes quickly and with much power, trying to unsteady Jesus, to shake up his confidence and his plans. First the Jewish leaders assault him with a huge lie in order to turn the people against him; then second, Satan strikes at Jesus' heart by creating panic and confusion about him among his own family. Both of these reactions are a sign of the 'Time' God has started, where God has begun the battle against sin, evil and death, and there is a violent reaction to God's way of achieving victory.

Questions: What sort of things might have been going through the minds of Jesus' family? What sort of things had he done which might worry them?

How would Jesus have felt about this attack from the Teachers of the Law?

How would he have felt about the misunderstanding from his family?

Which of these would have affected him more?

Who is really 'behind' all this confusion?

How does Jesus respond to this confusion?

What is the "eternal sin"; how did the Teachers "blaspheme" the Holy Spirit?

What does Jesus mean by his final statement, about brothers and sisters?

1. Assault from 'above' (v.22-30)

The Jewish authorities have been greatly embarrassed by the way Jesus put them in their place in the synagogue in front of many people (3:1-6). They are out to get him, because they are blind to the truth about him. So they make up a lie which is the greatest lie that could ever be told about Jesus. To call him 'Beelzebul' – the prince of demons (Satan himself!)- this is to look at something which is pure white and call it darkest black. What ***the teachers of the Law*** were doing was in fact Satan's work – what better way for Satan to hide himself and continue working secretly, than to divert the attention on to his greatest enemy, to try and get people to believe that

Jesus is Satan! What a clever trick that would be. So these teachers attack Jesus publicly with the most outrageous lie possible. There is a saying that often comes true: 'The bigger the lie, the more people will believe it.' That was how Adolf Hitler turned a nation to real madness. It's big lies like this that put fear into people's hearts and get people to lash out in defense. By pointing to Jesus and yelling "Satan! Satan!" they were probably hoping the people would stone him on the spot! But Jesus is quick to answer and show how ridiculous their claim is.

In the face of such fierce evil, which would strike terror into the heart of any human being, Jesus stands up to the attack. His most powerful weapon against such confusion and panic is the power of the ***truth***. How could Satan possibly be in the business of casting out his own forces? If that was true, he would be cutting his own throat; such an idea is ridiculous. Jesus' actions have actually been like a person robbing a strong man's house, tying up the demons (the 'strong man') and then taking their 'possessions' (v.27). Satan wouldn't do that to his own people. Jesus points out the truth of the matter in response to the teachers' stupid lie – it just doesn't make sense.

But then Jesus goes deeper, to the truth about what these teachers are really doing (v.28-30). For them to be saying 'white is black' when talking about Jesus, this is playing a dangerous game with God. What they are really saying is that miracles such as these are not being worked by God's Holy Spirit, but by Satan. This is giving credit to Satan for the miracle instead of God. For someone to say such a thing reveals their hard heart which is hell-bent on evil. They are refusing to see God at work. This is an unforgivable sin, an "eternal sin" (even the evil spirits themselves recognize the truth about who Jesus is! – see v.11).

This passage reminds us about Jesus' baptism, where he received the Holy Spirit. He is not working alone, but by the power of the Holy Spirit. And a lesson for us to learn from this is to be looking for what the Holy

Spirit is doing today, looking for God at work. Where is God working in your life? What are the 'demons' in your life that God is working to get rid of? Do you realize that the Holy Spirit will sort out the ***truth*** for you? Will you curse God for the disturbance this causes? Or will you praise him for battling on your behalf to set you free and bring you lasting peace?

2. Assault from 'below' (v. 20-21; 31-35)

The reaction of Jesus' own family was perhaps even more hurtful. It's one thing to be attacked by strangers; it's another to be deeply misunderstood by the people closest to you. They were being sucked in by the atmosphere of danger. Satan was being successful in confusing them and making them afraid for Jesus. In many ways their reaction is understandable, because over the previous weeks they had seen Jesus change so much: 1) He had thrown away his security as a carpenter, becoming a roving preacher with no income; 2) he had thrown away his safety by challenging the Jewish authorities; & 3) He had gone against the society he lived in by mixing with all sorts of undesirable people like tax-collectors. You could imagine Mary herself saying "What's happened to my boy? Has he gone mad?" like the people were starting to say (v.21). His family want to take him away from this dangerous situation where he is attracting too much of the wrong sort of attention. So they send a message for him to come out (v.31).

But Jesus will have plenty of time to explain things to them later. Right now he has a chance to make a point to the crowd about his relationship with them. He says in effect that the job he came to do extends beyond his own family to the whole world. He came to reach out to all people and make ***them*** his family, God's family. It's easy to imagine how in those days the eldest son would spend nearly all of his time looking after the interests of his immediate earthly family, taking on all the responsibilities for the family business or other work as the father grows older. Well that is not what Jesus came to do. Jesus came to be the brother of all people, the son who supports the family of all people – all people that is, who hear God's word and do it (v.35). This is something we should thank God for again and again, that God sent his own Son to be ***our*** brother – a big brother who puts his life on the line for us. We can completely depend on him because his love is 100%.

Again this section brings to mind Jesus' baptism, where his baptism by John (1:4-11) was not to wash away his own sins but to identify with us, to say "Yes, I willingly submit to being their brother, and to take their sins on my shoulders." So in the face of this subtle rejection even by his own family, Jesus doesn't retreat from the battle, like Satan is tempting him to do. Jesus knows well enough that his way of doing things is going to be rejected or misunderstood by everybody up until after his death and resurrection. He will be rejected again and again, because his way is God's way, not man's. Jesus stays on track to complete the mission his Father gave him.

How do you stand up to rejection and misunderstanding, even when it comes from your own family?

Reflect and pray: Dear Father, in a time where the truth is confused by so many voices that try to grab at our emotions, please preserve us. Thank you for sending your Son to be our brother. Please help us to see with clarity the truth about Jesus and the truth about your purpose for us. Help us to answer the objections and lies with calmness and insight that comes from you. Give us confidence in place of doubt and fear.

CHAPTER 3

Time to Understand

'Hear the Message'

Read **Mark 4: 1 - 20**

In chapter 3 the truth about Jesus is something that has been met with violent opposition from the Jewish authorities and Satan. The truth is a message about what God is doing in Jesus, and so Jesus sends his disciples to preach it (3:14). Why is it that some people ***hear*** the truth and their lives are changed, while others simply don't see the point? The story (or 'parable') that Jesus tells next explains why. It all has to do with people's hearts. Their hearts are either open to accepting God's word or their hearts are hard, wanting nothing to do with it. And Mark is most interested in opening up your heart as a reader, to hear this message he has to tell us about Jesus. This teaching is most important; it is vital that people hear the message about Jesus, and are saved - that is, God comes deep into your heart and changes your life.

Questions: Would you have understood the parable without the explanation Jesus gives?

Are the parables meant to make things easier to understand, or harder? Why?

Why does Jesus expect his disciples should have been able to understand?

What is the "secret of the Kingdom of God?"

Identify what the things in the parable really are: the sower, seeds, soil/path/rocks. Which of the 4 examples are surely Christians, and which are not?

Which one(s) are you?

1. A Nice Story - So What? (v.1-13)

If you told this parable (v.3-9) to someone in the street they would probably reply "Yeah, nice story - so what?" This is the sort of reaction Jesus was getting too. Even his disciples don't know what the parable means, and so they come to Jesus and ask him about it. He tells them they ***should*** understand his parables because "You have been given the secret of the kingdom of God." What secret? The truth about Jesus. As they follow him from place to place, watching him work and hearing him speak, he is the key to unlock their understanding about God's plan for the world. As their relationship with Jesus grows, so should their understanding grow, even when he speaks in parables. This is one of only 2 parables in the 4 Gospels which Jesus explains for us. Once you learn the meaning of this parable, you can easily 'unlock' the rest. The 'trick' is to correctly identify what each element of the parable represents. That's how parables work – they are a story that illustrates *something else.*

Jesus' explanation about ***why*** he speaks in parables (v.11b-12) is a bit shocking - it's so that most people ***don't*** understand. What Jesus is saying is that for most people, they are not interested in a relationship with Jesus or God at all. And they don't really ***want*** to hear the truth, because it is so powerful it might change them. So Jesus 'hides' the message in parables, which makes it even ***harder*** for these people to understand. Those who ***want*** to hear the message can do so, by coming to Jesus to ask for an explanation. It's the same for us - we're not expected to understand everything perfectly the first time we read God's word, but we can come and ask the teachers God has provided, as well as having the Holy Spirit to guide us personally.

2. The Explanation (v. 14-20)

The meaning of the parable is the most important thing for us to take in. God is doing his gentle work of spreading his 'word' through Jesus. This 'word' of course is the Good News about Jesus and God's Kingdom coming into the world. This is a word that brings life - great new life. God is spreading this word like a farmer sows seed, casting plenty of it around, to touch all people. God has done his part. After that, it is up to people to do theirs. Jesus says there are 4 possible ways people can respond to God's word:

Firstly, like a seed falling on a hard, flat path, people can be so hard-hearted that immediately Satan comes and snatches the word away from them. They want nothing to do with God's word; they want nothing to do with God. They ignore it, and prefer it to be eaten up, swallowed by the other gods, the evil things that rule their lives. This is so easy to see in our world. Just one example: Governments everywhere have given in like this, to the god of greed and gambling, to corruption for revenue and power. But not only them, but all the gamblers and investors out there who follow this example and think money can fix all their problems and make them happy. There are many other examples of this sort of thing all around us.

Secondly, like a seed that falls among the rocks, where there is a little bit of soil, some people hear the word of God in a 'shallow' way. They only half hear it, paying attention to the nice bits they want to hear, but don't accept the whole thing. So when trouble comes, when their faith comes up against some testing times, the word in them withers and dies - they give up. The truth hasn't sunk deep down into their hearts, for it to really grow strong. These are 'Christians' that you see who are all excited about God for a short time but then you don't see them again. You hear later that they have taken up something else, like crystals, or Hare Krishna, or ancestor worship or some such thing.

Thirdly, like seed that falls among thornbushes, there are Christians who are bound by something else as well as trying to hold onto God. They walk 2 paths at once. Sure, the roots of the seed go deep into the ground, but they let these other things grow equally as big in their lives. It might be their love for money, it might be pride in the work they do, it might be an addiction or temptation they (think they) can't live without. This is to try and hold on to 2 gods at once - the true one and a false one. All the good work that they could be doing for God is strangled - they won't 'produce a crop', they won't bear any fruit for the Lord. And their position before the Lord is therefore a scary one - Are they ***really*** faithful Christians, or not? Do they ***really*** live for the Lord who died for them, or do they live for themselves? Are they really saved, or not? In a lesser way, it's normal for Christians to sometimes feel like we're in this third category, where the pressures of life are crowding in on us. But that doesn't mean we have to give in, and let these things strangle our faith, our fellowship, or our witness. Jesus is encouraging us to stay focused on the word of God so we can keep the 'weeds of the world' under control instead of overcoming us.

Finally, the good soil stands for people who really take in the word of God and hold on to it. "Good soil" doesn't mean people who are already good - as Paul says in Romans, "All have sinned - no one is good, not one". Good soil is a person with an open heart, a heart that is ready to let God in. It's like soft soil that's been ploughed by the farmer. After the seed has been sown and the rain comes, the seed sinks down into the soil. And when the plant grows, it can sink its roots deep down and grow strong. We need to be like that soil, really desiring God to come into our heart, hungry for the truth and the life to grow in us. People who are open to God and looking for his ways to grow. These are the true people of God, who 'bear much fruit' (see John 15:1-17) The sort of crop, or fruit that we will produce will be a holy life, a good example to our friends and family, and sometimes even a witness with words about our faith in Jesus. This is living for the Lord, so that other people around us are able to see the word of God growing in us. This is the greatest purpose and joy for our lives - to be part of God's work just by living as Christians.

Reflect and pray: Which 'soil' are you? Open your heart, to hear God's word deeply in your life. Don't neglect those areas of your life where you struggle. The truth is that we all think of ourselves as being in more than one of these 'soils' from time to time. Jesus is not trying to 'categorize' us to judge us, but to prompt our thinking and prayer rather than skimming over the important stuff and making assumptions. God hears all your prayers and invites you every day to 'get real' with him, because the more we pray like this, the better we become at living the genuine Christian life.

'Hear the Message' no.2

Read **Mark 4: 21 - 34**

In the first part of chapter 4 we learn a lot about how to understand Jesus' parables. In the parable of the seeds (4:1-20) Jesus taught that people need to open their lives and accept God's word. This is the only way that God's word will grow in them and give them new life. To really ***hear*** God's word, a person must open their heart. So now is the time for a test - Can you hear God's message in these next 3 small parables? Jesus has implied in 3:11 that we should be able to, because "The secret of the kingdom of God has been given to you."

Questions: What is the main point, in each of the 3 parables?

What is the lamp, and when was it hidden away, and how is it now brought out into the open?

Who is the man, and what are the seed, the fruit, the mustard seed, the birds?

What is the point of Jesus' warning in v.24-25?

How is v.33-34 important for us?

1. A Lamp (v.21-25)

In this first parable the picture of a light or lamp is all about God's word, God's message, like in the previous parable. The truth about Jesus is not something to hide away; no-one puts a light under a bed, but out in the open. The truth about Jesus used to be hidden, before Jesus came, but now this truth shines brightly, for everyone to see. He is saying that he will openly tell this plain truth about God's plan, and no-one should try to cover it up. His disciples especially (including us) should want this message about Jesus to be clearly heard too, to shine out brightly to the people around us.

But then Jesus adds a word of warning (v.24-25). People who accept this word of God into their hearts will receive more, and really grow in their faith. But the person who is hard-hearted, who "has nothing", will have everything taken away - even his life. Jesus is saying that if we don't have God's word of life in us, then we will be judged - just the same way that we judge others around us. People everywhere think it's only fair to judge other people around them when they have done something wrong to them. They might have nothing to do with someone who has lied to them, or they might call the police if someone has stolen from them. Well it will also be fair for God to judge us because we have all wronged him through our sins. Jesus says, "Pay attention to what you hear!" because it is very important for us to hear the message of life which is offered to us through Jesus. Without this message, we will be judged by God, and that is a serious matter indeed.

2. A Growing Seed and a Mustard Seed (v.26-32)

What is the 'word' or 'message' all about, the message that Jesus wants people to pay attention to? It's all about the Kingdom of God coming into the world through Jesus. So Jesus starts teaching with parables to show what the Kingdom of God is like. The first one is much like the earlier parable of the seeds, except this time Jesus is raising the question of ***how*** the seed grows. The point Jesus is making is a very simple one - the Kingdom of God is the invisible work of ***God***. So if we think back to the seeds in the good soil being the word of God in a person's heart, it is the invisible work of God that ***makes*** the word grow powerfully in a person's life. It was very important for Jesus to explain this invisible Kingdom of God, this invisible work of God, because the people were expecting a very different kind of 'Kingdom'. They were expecting something like happened with King David in Old Testament times, where the kingdom of Israel was very powerful. They were expecting a new King David who would raise an army, kick out the Roman Empire and give Israel back their land again. Jesus was bringing a very different Kingdom - one much more powerful, a Kingdom that would rule in people's hearts, set people free from sin and give them a whole new life. That's the point of this parable - you won't see this Kingdom, you won't even see this power inside people that will change them, but you will see the person growing in their faith and life with God. You will see a holy life and a life that is prepared to witness to others about Jesus.

Jesus then adds a word of encouragement. A time will come for God to 'harvest' his people, to take them to himself. Jesus was probably thinking of all the truly faithful Israelites listening to him right there, who had heard the word of God from the Old Testament for a long time, and it had 'grown' in them, and now with Jesus speaking to them God was 'harvesting' his people. The 'Time' had come. But for us today there is also the time of Jesus coming again, the final harvest, when God will take all his faithful people to be with him forever, and give us new bodies like Jesus' resurrected body. God has promised that this time will come, and it will be a wonderful time for those who are his faithful people.

The second thing to learn about the Kingdom of God is that it is very big. It might look pretty small when you see just one person's life changing, but just like a tiny mustard seed (v.30-32), it is growing into the biggest of all. There will be plenty of people in God's Kingdom, just like a mustard tree can hold lots of birds. And this Kingdom will grow from a very small beginning - from one man dying and being buried in the ground like the mustard seed. It will grow to be the most magnificent place for people to live. And like the birds, we can find shelter and protection from everything in the world that seeks to attack or hurt us, in the safety of God's Kingdom. The Kingdom of God is the biggest, strongest, safest place to be.

3. Do You Get the Point? (v.33-34)

So do you see the way the parables work? They are picture language to show some very exciting things about God. Jesus always used parables (v.33). But then he was also very careful to explain the meaning clearly to his disciples. It's the same for us - the parables are supposed to make a simple but powerful point - but it's important to get the point right. So if you're not sure about their meaning, you should ask someone reliable to explain it, like the disciples did with Jesus.

Reflect and pray: That our loving Father would give us courage and faith to stand clearly before the world as Christians, without hiding it away. Pray for God's word to grow in you, and that your connection to all the others in this 'tree' would blossom, helping to build each other up. Give thanks for all this wonderful provision.

'Fear God & Have Faith'

Read **Mark 4: 35 - 5:20**

This last part of chapter 4 and all the events of chapter 5 have two things in common. 1) In each story people are afraid, filled with fear; 2) In each story Jesus shows incredible power. The large part of chapter 4 that we have just finished shows how Jesus was gently ***teaching*** the people about the Kingdom of God, but now up to the end of chapter 5 Jesus is putting the Kingdom of God into ***action***.

Questions: Why is Jesus so short with the disciples in the boat (v.40)?

How did his disciples feel in the boat, before they woke Jesus? How did they feel after he calmed the storm (v.41)? What is this a fear ***of?*** Is there a point being made here?

How do the demons feel about Jesus?

How do the people feel about this man, before Jesus helps him? How do they feel afterwards (v.15)?

Why might they be so afraid? How does Jesus calm their fear?

What is the point about 'territory' in v.10&17?

What is the overall message to us from these stories?

What sort of fears does God want to overcome in your life? How will he do that?

1. Fear of Nature, Fear of God. (4:35-41)

It is important to notice how Mark bothers to introduce this story with the words "On the evening of that same day." This storm on the lake happened on the same day that Jesus had been teaching about the Kingdom of God. He had said it was like a huge Mustard tree, a place of ***safety*** where God cares for his people and ***protects*** them (4:30-34). He has also told them about God's invisible ***power*** which makes this Kingdom grow (4:26-29). So when the disciples in the boat wake him up like a pack of frightened children, he is shocked. It's as if he's saying, 'Haven't you learned anything?' - "Why are you frightened? Do you still have no faith?"

They were afraid of the waves and losing their lives, when all they had to do was trust in God - he would look after them. God is much more powerful than anything; they should have faith in him. And so Jesus shows them God's power, with just a word. They are amazed, and now they are "***terribly*** afraid". Their fear of the waves is totally washed away by their fear of this man - he has the power of God. Only God can command the waters with a word and they obey. The disciples know this from the very first words of the Bible in Genesis chapter one, where God commanded the waters to separate from the land, and it happened. And the point for us is just the same - Fear God and have faith in Jesus - this will put out any other fears we might have. He is powerful to act whenever and wherever he chooses. If we are so upset with fear of things around us, then we are thinking of those things as being more powerful than God; this sort of thinking does not honour God. God doesn't want us to be paralyzed with fear of the things around us, he wants us to rather fear God and have faith in his Son Jesus. This fear of God is a good thing, because it gives us confidence to look to God's power to overcome the fears we have of things around us. If we had no fear of God's awesome power, then how could we have faith to pray to him for help?

(An interesting aside is to note how Mark tells us about the ***pillow*** Jesus was sleeping on. It is such an irrelevant detail to mention, and writers in those days, writing on papyrus, didn't waste ink or space on irrelevant things, so why is it there? The only logical explanation is that this is simply part of an eyewitness account of what actually happened. It does not appear in Matthew or Luke's account of this storm, so who is the eyewitness in the boat who relates this story to Mark (since Mark is not one of the twelve)? From other details about a John Mark in Acts, and the strange youth at the end of Mark's Gospel (14:51-52) it is a good guess that Mark is Peter's son, relating the bare facts just as his rough fisherman father would have done. It's things like this which give us great confidence about the ***accuracy and truth of these stories, happening just as Mark tells us they did***.)

2. Demons fear God, People fear God (5:1-20)

This event shows many things. One is that Jesus goes even to the most scary, unacceptable people. This man of Gerasa was afflicted by many demons and so he was cut off completely from society, from other people. This man today would spend all of his time in the Psychiatric Ward in a big Hospital. He was completely uncontrollable and very strong. Everyone was afraid of him, and had given up on him, but not Jesus. When the demons see Jesus, ***they*** are afraid; they scream in panic. They can see who he is, "The Son of the Most High God", just like the demon at the beginning of Mark (1:24). There are no limits to Jesus' power - he casts out a 'legion' of demons with a word.

Not only the demons, but the people from around there, when they saw this man sitting quietly, "they were all afraid"(v.15). This had been such an unsettling display of God's power that the demons and also the people beg Jesus' mercy for them to be able to cope with it. First the demons beg ***not*** to be cast out of that region, and later the people beg ***Jesus*** to leave that region. The details about the pigs help us understand what's happening here. This region and these people were very unacceptable to the Jews, because they farmed pigs, they ate pork, which is forbidden for Jews in God's law. These people would have thought of themselves as very much unacceptable to God because of this. So these people were very afraid indeed to see God working with such power among them. They were not God's people, so what could this power mean? It might be a sign of God's judgement on them. What might God do next? It was too terrifying for them to even think about, so they beg Jesus to leave. Jesus in his kindness agrees to, but commands the man to stay, so that the region might slowly come to understand that this was God blessing them, showing his love even for them - "Go back to your family and tell them how much the Lord has done for you and how kind he has been to you."(v.19) The demons are filled with fear for different reasons, but it's still the same fear of God. They had to be the worst, the lowest, most pitiful demons, for so many of them to pick on this one man. Life would be very hard for them 'out there' in the big world, so they beg not to be cast out of the region but prefer to go into the herd of pigs, to be imprisoned with them at the bottom of the lake.

All through these stories the fear of God, that is the fear of God's power in Jesus, brings a huge change in people. We are encouraged to fear God - it is a very good thing to fear God - because the fear of God builds faith in God, faith in his power to bless people and help people no matter what their situation might be. Fear of God is the most appropriate fear a human can have, because God is our Creator, not our mate. What are the things that fill you with fear, and stop you being the person God wants you to be? Is it the fear of not looking as nice as your friends? A fear of being rejected by them? The fear of not 'making it' in life like other people? The fear of taking responsibility for things, or committing yourself to something, in case you fail? Is it fear of people who have power over you? Or fear of losing your power over someone else? There are lots of things in this world which can fill us with fear. Don't fear the things around you, fear God instead, have faith in Jesus, who is much more powerful, and can overcome ***any*** of those fears!

Reflect and pray that God would overcome your common fears by the love and power of Jesus.

'Fear God & Have Faith' (part 2)

Read **Mark 5:21 - 43**

In this second half of chapter 5 two more groups of people are filled with fear - fear of God (in Jesus) - and they turn away from their other fears. The message is very similar - Have faith in Jesus and his awesome power, rather than being afraid of the things around you. God wants to build a solid faith inside us, for us to be strong and confident, to be able to hold our head up high and say, "Jesus is my protector, my Saviour, therefore I have no need to be afraid of anything". This sort of a life will give honour to God, instead of the other 'gods' in this world that we are often tempted to turn to, like sex, money, power, drugs, alcohol and social media. Better for us to look to the one true God, who is powerful to help us - all of us - from the lowest in society like this woman, to the highest like this man Jairus.

Questions: What sort of things might this woman have experienced in her life? Would she have been able to socialize in a Jewish community?

How would she have felt?

What would her position in society have been, with this ailment?

Why does Jesus want her to speak up when she is healed?

What things do you see in these two stories which are in common with last week's study?

What is the overall point of the passage?

What is Jairus' position in society?

Does Jesus expect any more or less from him than the woman? Why?

1. A Lowly Woman

Let's start with the woman in the middle of the story, since she is the first one Jesus attends to. If ever there was a person most rejected in the Bible, it's this woman. She is a Jew, and she has had a bleeding problem for 12 years. That means she is regarded as 'unclean' by Jewish Law. Nobody was allowed to touch her, and she would not be allowed into the temple to worship God. Also this means that she would not be able to touch her husband if she was married, and if she was not, it would be next to impossible for her to get married. She would also find it hard to live, because most employers would not give her a job, and "she had spent all her money" on trying to find a cure (v.26). Her life would have been very much separated from her family and friends, and as a woman she would have been even more looked down on, especially if this was a vaginal bleeding, like a permanent period. All sorts of nasty stories could have been made up about her. So this woman with a mere physical complaint is suffering terribly in body and mind and living in a great deal of fear about many things - fear about her future, fear of being rejected, and fear about never getting well. With all this fear inside, she is driven in desperation to reach out secretly and touch just the corner of Jesus' coat. There is something powerful happening inside this woman even before she touches Jesus, and it's called ***faith***. God has touched her heart, so that she knows deep down that if she does this she will be healed. And notice how she has only "***heard*** about Jesus" (v.27), which is the same for us.

But for this woman to be completely healed Jesus wants two more things for her: 1) for her to be healed of her many fears, to be able to stand tall in front of everybody and publicly say "God has healed me - so don't you people reject me anymore" and 2) for her to give praise and thanks to the one true Healer from God - Jesus, and to fear him, and stand up and say it publicly, rather than hiding what God has done through him. Both of these things are achieved when Jesus turns around and asks who touched him, knowing that power had gone out from him. What a dramatic scene! Imagine the power of this scene if you were watching it on film, hearing all the thoughts going through this woman's mind! Imagine the fear of God she experienced when Jesus calls out, knowing what she had done, and getting her to confess what had happened. She is filled with the greater fear of God, as "she came, trembling with fear" (v.33). But she is also filled with faith, and she finds an accepting, understanding, loving Jesus who recognizes this as he says, "My daughter, your faith has made you well. Go in peace and be healed of (all) your trouble."(v.34)

The example of this woman's faith is directly opposite to the disciples in the boat at the end of ch.4. God wants us to be like this woman - hearing the message about Jesus and being filled with the fear of God and faith in Jesus, to completely change our lives, to be healed, to be saved. The original word used in verses 28 & 34 for "get well" is the same word for "saved", so can be translated "If I just touch his clothes I will be saved" and "Your faith has saved you". The point is that Jesus is not just interested in our physical healing, but our complete salvation - a new, open relationship with God through the powerful work of his Son Jesus.

2. A Highly Positioned Man

This man Jairus is completely opposite to the woman when it comes to his position in society. He is a man, he is a wealthy acceptable Jew, and he is an official of the synagogue (a religious leader). ***But Jesus expects the very same thing from him as was shown by the woman*** -"Don't be afraid, only believe"(v.36)

Like the woman, this man had to realize the hopelessness of other forms of help and turn to Jesus. He too had to stand in front of other people and confess his faith in Jesus. He too faced rejection, from all the other Jewish leaders, by putting his faith in Jesus. But he also was desperate, for the life of his daughter. And the miracle Jesus performs here is the greatest of all - bringing the dead back to life. It's something to strike the greatest fear of God into the hearts of all who witnessed it, and of course it shows that if Jesus has power over death here, then he has power over death for all of us too - that is what he promises elsewhere for all who believe in him - resurrection from the dead and eternal life when he returns one day.

So from the lowest person to the highest person, Jesus wants the same for all of us, he doesn't play favourites but loves us all the same. He wants us to fear God and have faith in Jesus. Jesus is the one who God has given all power to, so that we should not fear anything else, whether it be people, sickness or even death. Jesus has power over all things, and can do everything just right for those who trust in him. We don't always get this right, we make mistakes, but the more we trust in Jesus the stronger we are. These stories encourage us to be more like the woman and Jairus, and less like the disciples in the boat.

Reflect and pray: express your fears to God, your hopes, your hurts, your difficulties. Pick just the two or three most pressing matters and surrender them into the loving hands of Jesus. Ask him to heal and forgive, to give you a new outlook on life. Ask him to give you new strength and possibilities, with the confidence to move forward, knowing his presence with you.

'Faith is Costly'

Read **Mark 6: 1 - 13**

After the previous four examples of faith in Chapter 5, here are 2 more which tell us something more about faith - faith is not understood by many people close to us, and to have faith in God means really depending on God. To put it another way, faith costs a lot - it can sometimes cost you your family, friends, and even your possessions.

Questions: Why do Jesus' townsfolk reject him? What is blocking their acceptance of him? How does this sort of thing happen in our lives?

How can Mark say that Jesus "***was not able*** to perform any miracles there"?

Why is faith so important for people to understand who Jesus is?

Why do you think the rejection of Jesus is highlighted so much in Mark's Gospel? Can you remember another occasion in Mark when this same sort of thing happened?

Did Jesus give up, when he was rejected?

What do you do when you are rejected in some way for your faith?

How important is ***teaching***, for our faith (v.2, 6, 12)?

Why did Jesus send the disciples out with so little?

What does this mean for us in our daily lives?

1. Jesus rejected - not much faith at home

Earlier on we saw how Jesus was rejected by the religious leaders, and also in a subtle way, by his family (3: 20-35). Likewise in this story Jesus is rejected by his own home town. They had known him as 'just a carpenter's son'. There is a theme of rejection which runs through Mark's Gospel, and it's important for us to pay due attention to it. The reason why the townsfolk rejected him was "the people did not have faith"(v.6). They had no doubt about what he could ***do,*** in terms of his wonderful wisdom and miracles (v.2) - they had all heard the reports about him, they had heard him speak in the synagogue (v.2) and some had witnessed these things for themselves. It was rather a matter of believing this all ***meant something*** important. They might believe what he did really happened, but they were not prepared to believe ***in*** him, there was no fear of God when they were near him. They were not prepared to honour him and worship him like the disciples had in the boat, or the woman who touched his coat, or Jairus had done, because these townsfolk had known him all his life as a lowly carpenter. Jesus knew this was a common thing that happened to prophets - people sent by God - it happened all through the Old Testament times. This incident shows just one more of the barriers to people's faith - 'He can't be the King of the Jews, the Messiah we've been waiting for, he's just a carpenter's son'.

What do you think of Jesus? If you too reject God's chosen way of sending his King as a lowly servant, then you too will not experience "any miracles" (v.5) because of your lack of faith in him; you may miss out on the love and power and the new life he has to offer. All the way through the Gospel story we see people ***rejecting*** Jesus. It's very sad, but it's also necessary, because God is not going to ram Jesus down our throats. We can either accept Jesus or reject him. And the cost for us might be like the cost for Jesus - that when we put our trust in Jesus we are rejected by our friends and family too.

In what ways have you experienced some level of rejection for being a Christian, from family, friends and workmates? How do you respond at these times? God doesn't want us to cringe back, but to stand firm, to show a confidence in the face of such adversity, which will have an effect on those who see us. This doesn't mean we become offensive or judgmental, but quite the opposite - by maintaining a witness of quiet, loving faithfulness when we are mocked for our faith or being pressured to give up something important to us (like attending church), it is amazing how often people gain a new respect for us. Jesus doesn't give in to his family or townsfolk when they misunderstand him - he kept right on going, aware of the greater mission of love he had under God his Father and for the benefit of those people. It is exactly the same for us as Christians. It is amazing how often the most unlikely people, who are even violently opposed to Christianity, are eventually converted through the persistent, loving witness of a Christian. People like the Apostle Paul, who was having Christians imprisoned, and gave his assent to the stoning of Stephen! People like St Augustine, who in the 4th century lived a horrible life of immorality, but whose mother prayed earnestly for him for many years, and he became one of the greatest Christian writers. We can indeed have an effect on people around us, if we lovingly persist - there is no greater experience as a Christian than to be part of God's saving work, where God works through your witness to bring a person to Christ - this is something we are ***all*** invited, equipped and encouraged to do, through a simple, trusting faith in the living Jesus.

2. The disciples sent - have faith 'away from home'

The second story shows what sort of faith Jesus expects from his disciples. He expects them to depend on God rather than depending on their own resources, 'the things of home', so to speak. He expects them to put their faith into action. They were to take only the bare minimum they needed to carry and then trust in God to provide the rest.

It is also important to notice how Jesus had again been ***teaching*** (v.6), and he sends out his disciples to cast out evil spirits and to "***preach*** that people should turn away from their sins" (v.12). People are expected to respond in faith to the word they hear. And a real change is expected in their lives. Again we see how physical healing and spiritual healing go together. The disciples are sent out to do a complete ministry, not just the nice and exciting bits. Faith is not just some fuzzy feeling, designed to simply warm the cockles of our heart. God wants complete salvation for people, nothing less.

The problem of human sin, the problem of rejecting God's way, is the root of all human problems, and that is the part which Jesus is really coming to tackle, in order to permanently repair the 'human condition' as we call it, both right now and even more completely in the end. The challenge right now is for us to turn away from our sins, to put our faith in the way that God has done things in Jesus, and to trust in his ability to provide for us. Then we will know and experience his salvation, his healing in our lives. And we too will be sent out with a new purpose in life, to serve him and love people around us.

Reflect and Pray: In what ways is God asking you to exercise your faith right now? It may very well be that this will involve giving something up, to show more completely his power to provide everything you need. Pray for the Helper – the Holy Spirit, to be prompting you and equipping you in your everyday life, to be able and willing to stand out for Jesus when opportunities arise. And when you get it wrong – as all of us do sometimes – be ready to talk to God about that also, knowing his forgiveness is always at hand, ready to get you back on your feet again and well-positioned for the next challenge!

CHAPTER 4

Community Life Explained

'Tragedy points forward'

Read **Mark 6: 14 - 29**

The death of John the Baptist is a very clear pointer to what lies ahead for Jesus. John and Jesus are 'connected' in their mission from God. They are like 2 sides of a hinge the centre hinge of all history where John is the last of the Old Testament prophets and Jesus is the first of something entirely new. Jesus will die a terrible death like John, but whereas John is just a man, Jesus will explode back into new life, crashing the gates of hell and death, to open up glory for others to follow. So, this death of John is like a dress rehearsal for the main event coming up later.

Questions: What sort of person do you think Herod is? Why is he so worried? Is he a dangerous person to be noticing Jesus?

What is the connection between this story and last week's study?

Picture the scene in Herod's palace; what are the elements of a Shakespearian play that you see here?

What do you think Jesus' reaction might have been to the death of John?

Can you think of a modern movie where one of the heroes gets the chop, and his partner is spurred on with more focus and determination?

If John and Jesus are examples for us to follow, then how will you stand up to people who give you a hard time for being a Christian?

When might you need to stand up for what is right, and face the consequences?

1. Rejection builds up

So far in Mark's Gospel Jesus has been rejected by the Jewish authorities, his own family, and his own hometown. Now King Herod, the Mr. Big of the ruling authorities in the land takes an interest in Jesus. This is a dangerous man who now rejects him. And a dangerous man is most dangerous when he is scared. Herod is quite disturbed when he hears about what Jesus is doing. The focus of the story is on Jesus, and we hear about Herod's reaction to Jesus first, even though it was some time after the death of John. With this story a new level of tension and danger enters the story. Herod had been scared of John because he knew John was from God, but at the whim of a dancing girl Herod still killed him. Now Herod "heard about all this" that Jesus had been doing and saying, and that scared him too, thinking it was John raised from the dead. Even the pagan King Herod could see the connection between John and Jesus, that they were both prophets preaching the same message of repentance.

Also notice how Jesus & John stand up to rejection and danger. They don't compromise their message to save their own skins. This too is an example for us as Christians, where in many countries of the world Christian communities are persecuted for their faith, persecuted for standing up for what is right, and persecuted for their message, which is unpopular when seen alongside the world's views and values. This is an essential element of life in any Christian community, even ours.

2. A Dress Rehearsal

I find it helpful sometimes in Mark to imagine I'm watching this as a movie. Today some movies are very good at capturing the exciting drama of a story. In this story, the scene with John the Baptist is one of the most dramatic, chilling scenes. And like in a good movie, there are a number of high points which build up to the climax at the end. This is one of those high points, which makes the climax at the end ring with memories of what happens here to John This story is a classic tragedy like Shakespeare's 'Macbeth'. There is forbidden love, with Herod's marriage to his brother's wife. There is the pomp and wealth of Herod's palace, and young beauty with Herodias' dancing daughter. There is the big man who makes a foolish mistake which turns his face from happy celebration to grey dread when he sees he is trapped into killing John. And there is the jealousy, guilt and sneakiness of the ruthless woman, to get rid of the man who is pointing out her shame. Finally, there is violent death, with the bloodied head of John delivered on a plate.

This scene is like we find in many movies, where the lesser partner tragically dies and the real hero is spurred on to complete his mission. The death of his friend makes him even more determined to go on. John and Jesus had real partnership in their work, and John made it very clear that Jesus was greater than he. He'd said, "I am not worthy even to untie his sandals" and " I must decrease, and he must increase" (John 3:30). Jesus too knew that John was the greatest prophet from the Old Testament age "There has not been anyone greater than John the Baptist, yet the lowest person in the Kingdom of Heaven is greater than he" (Matthew 11: 11). John and Jesus are both great in God's mission. But both die terrible deaths. After John's death, Jesus is all alone. And he is more focussed on meeting his own end. That is where the great victory will take place, not through winning power like the world wins power, but through dying. It is the power of God in him, obedient and full of love, giving up his life for others, that has the greatest power ever known. It is his power to bring in the New Testament age, the Kingdom of Heaven, where even the lowest of us can become children of God, brothers and sisters with Jesus. This is what makes us, Christians, greater than even John the Baptist.

Reflect and Pray: How deeply important does it make you feel, when you realise this tragic drama has been played out (for real) for your benefit?

'If only they would see!'

Read **Mark 6: 30 - 56**

In these 3 stories Mark gets back to his main purpose for writing his book, which is to show how important it is to ***have faith in Jesus***. Mark has many stories about the amazing things Jesus ***did,*** to encourage us to have faith in Jesus, to depend on him and trust in him. These 3 stories show Jesus' great love for people, and how he had great compassion. But the people at this time did not understand what was going on. They were like blind people who could not see what was really happening right in front of them. And so they didn't have faith. When we read these stories, ***we*** can understand, because Mark helps us.

Questions: What is it about the feeding of the 5,000 that the disciples were supposed to have learned (v.52)? What stopped their understanding?

Do you know any Old Testament stories where God's people were miraculously fed? What was the main point of those stories?

What is the 'connection' between Jesus and Moses?

Which is more important, people being fed or being taught?

Why do you think Jesus was intending to walk ***past*** the boat?

Why did he 'change course' and get in the boat? Is Jesus just showing off? What do you think about the crowd's motivation & level of understanding at this time?

Does your Christian community operate like the crowds in this section of Mark? Explain your answer.

1. Trusting in Jesus

Earlier in chapter 6 Jesus sent out his 12 disciples, the apostles, to cast out demons, preach repentance and heal people. Now in verse 30 they return and "told him all they had done and taught". And that's all Mark says about it. Mark doesn't say anything about what they did, because the focus is on Jesus. Jesus is the one who sent them out; they went on his authority and with his power, not their own.

This is important in the story, because it explains one of the things that stops the apostles from understanding. The feeding of the 5,000 is a great miracle, and the point is that ***Jesus*** made it happen. When Jesus tells the disciples to share out the bread and the fish, they are very excited about what happens, but they probably think ***they*** are doing this miracle. They had been doing great things while they were sent out by Jesus before this, and now they thought that was continuing. They were filled with pride in themselves, thinking they were something special. But in fact it was God doing something special through Jesus. Their faith is supposed to be focused on Jesus, to adore him and praise God for what Jesus is doing. As Mark points out after Jesus walks on the water "they had not understood the real meaning of the feeding of the 5,000, their minds could not grasp it." This last bit should be translated "their hearts were hardened". They did not see the truth of what was happening because their hearts were hardened, they were filled with pride in themselves. They needed to open their hearts and trust in Jesus, instead of looking inside themselves and thinking these things were their own achievements. And it is the same with us. If we are looking to praise God for what Jesus has done and what Jesus is doing in our lives, then we are seeing and understanding correctly. But if we keep looking to ourselves and other things for strength then we are not living in faith, and God can do very little with us and in us. This is the second indispensable element for life in a Christian community – humility, focusing on what God is doing rather than what we are doing.

2. Feeding the 5,000 - wow!

This miracle shows Jesus' ***love and compassion*** for the people. This collection of people were fast becoming a community; they had come together to hear him, it was late, and they were hungry. Rather than make them leave, he feeds them. But what was he most concerned about? Not that they were hungry, but that "they were like sheep without a shepherd" (v.34). They were without direction in their lives, they were searching for happiness and peace of mind, comfort for all their troubles in life, and they had no-one to guide them. They had no-one to 'feed their minds' with the word of God. "So he began to ***teach*** them many things". This is much more important than just food in the stomach. The reason why he fed them was so they could stay and hear more of his teaching, so they didn't have to leave so soon.

The Old Testament often relates how God's community was destroyed because the leaders were bad shepherds; this was happening again in Jesus' time. The Pharisees and other religious leaders were getting things terribly wrong. The people needed to be fed with the truth about God, and so they were very attracted to the teaching of Jesus. In John's Gospel, chapter 10, Jesus calls himself the Good Shepherd, and this is promised in Isaiah 40 and Ezekiel 34, how the bad shepherds will be replaced by God himself as the shepherd of his people, developing God's people God's way.

The miracle itself is a sign of this same thing, because such a miracle was also performed by the 2 good shepherds of the Old Testament, Moses and Elijah. Moses was leader in the desert after the Exodus, and God rained down manna (bread) from the sky to feed the people for 40 years before they entered the promised land. And Elijah at one point during a great famine survived on a jar of oil and a jar of flour which never ran out (1 Kings 17). So when Jesus does this great miracle of feeding 5,000 people with a few loaves which don't run out, it is like both of those stories from the Old Testament, and this should have been ringing in the minds of everyone there, because they all knew these stories. The disciples, who could see what was happening to the bread, should have known what was going on here - the new Moses had come, the one God had promised to send (Deut.18:14-19). They should have been overcome with fear and worship to God.

3. Walking on Water - wow!

The second miracle is another opportunity for the disciples to trust Jesus in relation to the water and the wind. They failed in their faith at the end of chapter 4, now something similar happens. At the end of the day Jesus sends the people home and goes off alone to pray. Notice how important prayer is for Jesus. If he needs to pray, then we need to even more. Jesus praying shows how he trusted in God for everything. The Disciples have gone ahead, across the lake again in the boat and they are having a difficult time, rowing against the wind. Jesus sees this and walks out on the water to them. Mark says, "he was going to pass them by". He was going to let them see him, for them to trust in him and supposedly the wind would have died down. It doesn't take much imagination to see him then continue across and meet them on the other side. But what does happen? They don't even recognize him; they think he's a ghost. Their faith is so weak that they still don't accept the sort of things he can do. And so he stops to calm them down and steps into the boat. ***How hard it is to for these disciples to put their faith in Jesus!*** And so Mark adds the comment about how they had learned nothing from the feeding of the 5,000. They should have learned from that experience that this is God doing extraordinary, powerful things that match the time of the Exodus. The realization of such an enormous event should have inspired real faith in Jesus, with eyes to see the truth about him.

4. The Crowds - wow!

Crowds of people are flocking around Jesus, both here and in the last section where he is healing lots of people from all over the region. The crowds seem to recognize that someone great is working in their midst. They are coming for healing, for teaching, to see great miracles, and they're all very excited (much like church communities today). Mark is telling us something by mentioning these crowds. He wants us to notice how so many people want something from him, so many people seem to love him, at this stage. He's doing just what they want him to do - giving them lots of attention and making them feel good. But Mark wants us to see how they don't really understand anything about him - they are not really interested in having faith in God, they are just interested in getting what they want right now. Later in the story, when he is before the court being sentenced to death, and he's just letting it happen, the crowd soon turns against him and calls for him to be executed. Are you just one of the crowd, along for the excitement, or are you one of the few who truly understands, who sees God's plan in Jesus' death for your sins, who feeds on Jesus' teaching, filling your heart with God's love and responding with real love for God?

Reflect and Pray: What sort of things are you anxious about in your life - things out of your control, like the wind and the waves were for the disciples in the boat - where God wants you to trust in his provision, and pray, giving some credit for who he really is? God wants to completely change our lives from the inside out, but that can only happen if we put our trust in Jesus. And this is essential for living in Christian community, whether it's a small one like in the boat or a large one like on shore.

'Get Real with God!'

Read **Mark 7: 1 - 23**

As we have seen so far in this Gospel, Mark concentrates on the important things a person must understand if they want to be a true Christian. The most important teaching up until now has been 'Have faith in Jesus and open your heart to the word of God'. This next section flows on from that, becoming slightly more challenging. The contrast between the attitudes of the religious authorities and other regular people who have genuine faith becomes even starker. And this interaction has lessons for us, about how to live in Christian community.

Jesus is in effect saying: 'Get real with God you might fool people by putting on a show, making out you are a good person, but you can't fool God (or me).' Jesus knows that if a person really believes in him and the word of God, then there will be a deep desire from the person's heart to live the way God wants them to. They will want their lives to be pure 'from the insideout', because love for God has taken over their hearts, where there used to be selfishness and greed. This is how the Bible from beginning to end expects people to worship God. You can't pretend to worship him; you can't hide what is really in your heart. But the Pharisees try to.

Questions: Why do you think the Pharisees were so determined to 'nit-pick' about the Law, with people around them? Why didn't Jesus do this? What have the Pharisees got wrong?

How are our lives truly made clean?

What sorts of things can get in the way of us having a cleansed conscience?

What is Jesus doing with the Old Testament Law? Is he throwing it out altogether?

What is the purpose of Jesus overturning the food laws?

How might we do 'religious duties' which put us in the same basket as the Pharisees?

How might/should/can we avoid this?

1. The Pharisees condemned (v.1-13)

It is a sad fact that people often take the good religion of God and twist it to suit themselves. They often take one part of the Bible and blow it out of all proportion to the rest, because it says what they want to hear, but ignore the parts they don't like. This turns God's rich, powerful and true religion into a manmade one. God hates this, and Jesus hated it when he saw the religious leaders of his day doing it (the Pharisees). They were so hung up on certain rules in the Old Testament that they lost the true meaning of what the Old Testament is about. It's really about the long sad history of God with his people how God works again and again to bless them, but these people have hearts that are hard and closed instead of being open to God, where they were expected to trust in him and love their neighbour. The Pharisees are continuing that sad history because they think that by simply doing all the right rituals, they are okay with God. And what's worse, they try to force other people to be like them. But these laws about cleaning hands and cups and bowls are small stuff compared to the more important things like hate and jealousy and greed in their hearts. These sorts of things are a much bigger problem in a person's relationship to God. But they think they are okay so long as they 'do the right thing'.

Jesus treats all of the Bible as the word of God, not just the first five books of the Bible, like the Pharisees were doing. Jesus knew that in Isaiah's time, much later than Moses, the people were thinking and doing just the same as the Pharisees. Jesus uses the words from Isaiah to condemn the Pharisees: "These people, says God, honour me with their words, but their heart is really far away from me. It is no use for them to worship me, because they teach manmade rules as if they were my laws. "(v.67) True worship of God is not just following certain 'outside' rules, but must start in a person's heart. A person needs to be honest with God about their own sin, so they are not so proud and sure of themselves that all they do is condemn other people. God made us to bless and serve other people out of love for God. This is the true 'doing' part of worship which the Pharisees had forgotten. So how do you worship God? Do you love to hear him talking to you through the Bible, and love to serve other people, because of his great love for you? Or do you limit your worship to just doing a few 'religious' things, which doesn't really honour God at all? When you live in a Christian community, it should be permeated through and through with God's love and grace.

2. The Disciples are encouraged to live differently (v.14-23)

Jesus tries to explain all this 'in a nutshell' for the crowd in v. 15. But even his disciples don't quite get the point. It isn't what goes into a person that makes them "unclean" (that is, unholy, or rotten), but rather the 'dirty' thoughts that come out of a person's heart and makes them do sinful things. This makes their whole body 'unclean' in God's eyes.

If a person wants to be truly clean with God, they have to let God clean them from the 'inside-out'. This is the true meaning of these Old Testament laws. God's people are to live the good way God wants them to, with their actions coming from a pure heart, not covering up your sins but owning up to God and letting him change you bit by bit each day. These Old Testament laws were supposed to show how God's people were different; they were holy, and '*separated, set apart*' from the evil world around them. This is especially the purpose of the food laws, designed to show the world Israel's extra dependence on God. So, this was a practical way of living separated from the ways of the world around them. But now Jesus is showing that God's people are going to be even more different, made pure from the *inside,* and no longer separated from the world but living in the world, mixing with all sorts of people as God's ***different, holy*** people. This is why Jesus overturns the food laws they are no longer valid because God's blessing is now going out to all the nations of the world through Jesus, without the old divisions anymore. The true and powerful signs of holiness now are from a truly cleansed heart, through the power of Jesus, working out into *every* aspect of our lives. So how is your heart? Wanting to be open, so your whole life can be more pure, more holy? Or maybe covered up, hiding from the truth?

Note also the New Testament letter to the Hebrews, 10: 12-14, 19-22, where after the death & resurrection of Jesus, the way for us to be made "clean" is now possible:

"But when this priest (Jesus) had offered for all time one sacrifice for sins, he sat down at the right hand of God. By one sacrifice he has made perfect forever those who are ***being made holy*** ...

Therefore, brothers & sisters, since we have confidence to enter the most holy place by the blood of Jesus, by a ***new and living way*** opened for us through the curtain, that is, his body ... let us draw near to God with a sincere heart in full assurance of faith, having our ***hearts sprinkled to cleanse us*** from a guilty conscience."

Reflect and pray: How is your conscience, these days? How is your heart? Open to God? Maybe you've been living a life of hiding behind all your good deeds, but underneath it's not so good. Pray that the Lord of Life will fill you with new life, to truly live his way.

'Unclean' People!'

Read **Mark 7: 24 - 37**

In the first part of chapter 7 we saw how Jesus challenged people to 'get real' with God. Any religion where you put on a show on the ***outside*** and pretend to be a Christian is very dangerous. God sees ***inside,*** into our hearts, and he does not want us to be hypocrites, where our words and actions hide what is really going on. God wants us to know him and worship him honestly. This is what makes our hearts clean, having God come into us and change our lives. Jesus pointed out to the religious leaders that it's not food or anything else that goes into us that makes us 'unclean', but the evil things that ***come out of our hearts*** that make us unclean before God. Now Jesus meets an 'unclean' woman whose daughter has an "unclean" spirit, and he turns our thinking upside-down about them too. Both stories show how 'unclean' people become clean, accepted by God, through Jesus.

Questions: Why did Jesus at first resist helping this woman? (Who are the "children" and "dogs" in his little parable?) What changed his mind?

Notice the footnote in v.25, how the word "evil" is literally "unclean"; How does this word (and so the whole story) relate back to the previous study?

Who, really, is unclean - the Pharisees from the section before, or this woman and her daughter? Why?

What would the Pharisees have thought about the deaf & dumb man's condition? Why would they be wrong?

Do you know why Tyre and Sidon are significant places for Jesus to be doing such miracles? What is this a sign of, or how is it a preparation for what is to come after Jesus' death and resurrection?

With these stories in mind, how do we come to Jesus?

1. An Unclean Woman and Spirit (v.24-30)

The thing that stands out in this story is the way it contrasts with the first part of chapter 7. This woman is doing the exact opposite to what Jesus was denouncing in the previous story. This woman was regarded by the Jews as 'unclean', because she was not a Jew but a Gentile, and the evil spirit which has possessed her daughter should really be called an ***"unclean"*** spirit, because that's the word Mark uses. The woman is 'unclean', but what ***comes out of this woman's heart*** is a wonderful faith in Jesus. Jesus says to her that "because of your answer", that is, because of what she says from her heart, Jesus heals her daughter. And what a loving person Jesus is, to respond to the desperate plea of this mother!

Jesus seems to speak to this woman harshly at first, but that's because he knows that he is supposed to concentrate his ministry on the Israelites, the Jews who were God's special people. Jesus had come to fulfil everything in the Old Testament, to complete all the promises God had made to his people over thousands of years. But Jesus also knew that his work on earth was going to extend God's blessings out to the whole world. So he is prepared to make an exception with this woman, because she is so persistent and faithful, and because this is a sign of what's to come after Jesus' death and resurrection. Look at her faith! She knows that just a 'crumb' of God's blessing is enough to heal her daughter. Look at her humility! She is prepared to accept this picture of herself as a ***dog***, just as the Jews of her day used to called them "Gentile dogs". She knows that she is not worthy of such attention from God.

She is a woman who is truly open-hearted and honest before God. But she also knows that the loving God in Jesus will not turn her down, so she ***keeps asking*** rather than turning away. Jesus is gently testing her out when he says, "Let us first feed the children; it isn't right to take the children's food and throw it to the dogs". He's not really trying to be insulting, but he wants her to realize her place, that by God's choice the Jews had been his people for 2,000 years, and Jesus had to 'feed them' first. What makes the difference is her humility. She accepts her humble place in God's plan and so Jesus blesses her greatly.

How should your heart be, when you come to the Lord? Humble. Every one of us are unworthy to receive God's blessings, because we have all rebelled against him and sinned terribly. But when we open our hearts humbly to him and admit that we are terrible, deserving nothing - then he can gently but powerfully rebuild our hearts and lives. Nothing is beyond his power, if we get our hearts right. He heals this woman's daughter without even being anywhere near her; she's at home.

2. Tyre and Sidon, another healing (v.31-37)

Jesus met the woman "near the city of Tyre". Now Mark tells us Jesus "went through Sidon". This is not just a coincidence when Mark points out what happened in these places. These places in Old Testament times were the most evil, sinful places, often at war against Israel. They were the real baddies. In the Old Testament there are many times when God's prophets announced curses and judgement on these places because they were so evil. So when Jesus goes through them, bringing blessing and healing, it's a sign that God is spreading his blessing outside Israel now, out into even the most sinful world. When Jesus blesses people in these towns, he is showing that no matter how sinful or terrible a person's life may have been, God wants to heal them and give them new life.

The Jews would have said this man was deaf and dumb as a sign of God's judgement on him and the rest of Sidon. But Jesus shows that even all those generations of evil from the past, plus whatever sin this man may have committed in his life - all of this was now being met by God's love and healing in Jesus. Jesus accepts and heals anybody, no matter what their background is. And Jesus breaks down the barriers between different races of people, for all of us to be God's new community, God's family together. Jesus turns these signs of God's judgement - deafness and dumbness - into signs that God's Kingdom has come to bless all the world. This is just what the prophet Isaiah wrote in the Old Testament:

"The blind will be able to see, and the deaf will hear. The lame will leap and dance, and those who cannot speak will shout for joy… Those who the Lord has saved will travel home... singing for joy.

They will be happy forever, free from sorrow and grief" (35:5&10)

As Jesus said in Chapter 1: "The time has come, the Kingdom of God is near!", and as Paul says in one of his letters, "This is the hour to receive God's favour; today is the day to be saved!"(2 Corinthians 6:2)

Reflect and Pray: Open your heart and be healed, be changed - no matter where you have come from, what you have been through, or how bad you think you might be. God loves you and wants to bless you. But that can only happen if you are honest and open with him, with a humble heart.

'Not Like Pharisees'

Read **Mark 8: 1 - 21**

Here is another story where Jesus feeds a crowd by a miracle, and then he expects his disciples to have ***learned*** something from it, just like in chapter 6. What is happening here must be so, so important. It's all about seeing Jesus as ***the Lord***. He is the Lord of all the universe his miracles show that. He is the Messiah the Jews were all waiting for. But some things stand in the way of people seeing this. The big obstacle in this story is a person's own pride. If a person is too proud about themselves, then they can't be ***humble*** enough to come under Jesus' control, to submit to him as their Lord. They can't bow down to him and let ***him*** run their life. Pride is something that affects all of us, from the richest to the poorest. It's when we stubbornly refuse to see that we need God's help. It's when we say, "I'm okay I can live without Jesus right now", when in fact we do need him very much.

Questions: Why have the disciples missed the point of the miracle this second time?

What is the "yeast of the Pharisees and Herod"?

How does pride often affect us as Christians, and what sorts of things tempt us away from trusting in Jesus?

Why did Jesus feed the people?

Why are the disciples thinking about their stomachs instead of hearing the spiritual things Jesus says to them (v. 16 - 17)?

How does this often happen to us? What can we do to avoid it?

When does it finally sink in for these disciples that Jesus is really the Lord of the universe?

When did it sink in for you?

1. The Pharisees (v.11-13)

The Pharisees are the number one example of people who are filled with pride. They think Jesus should do what they want, when in fact they should be doing what he wants. Their pride stops them from believing the reports about his miracles. Their hearts are so hard and closed, and so they expect him to do a miracle just for them, to prove who he is. Jesus makes it very clear that they will be shown no miracles, because miracles are only for those who have hearts open to God humble people who know they need God's help. Lots of people are like this today. They say, "If Jesus is really Lord, then let's see him do a miracle for me, then I'll believe." They say this because they are so confident in the other things around them. They are so confident in money, or medical science, or their own abilities, that they say, "I'm okay I don't need God." They are proud in themselves and the things they can buy to help them. And even poor people sometimes do the same in our western world today, trusting in doctors and money (a win on the pokies) or alcohol or ripping off social security for all they can, thinking "I can get whatever I need I don't need to hand it all over to Jesus."

2. Jesus warns the disciples (v.14-21)

Jesus wants his people to learn from the Pharisees' bad example, and not to follow them. He says, "Take care, and be on your guard against the yeast of the Pharisees and Herod". Yeast (the stuff that makes bread rise) is a picture from the Old Testament that the Jews knew well. It was a picture of sin. Every year at the time of Passover, the Jews would sweep the house out, to get rid of all the little bits of yeast, and they made only flat bread without yeast. It was to remind them that they were supposed to clean up their lives, sweep out all the sin. But why this picture of yeast? Because the sin that leads to all other sin is pride, and pride 'puffs up' a person like yeast puffs up bread. Pride puffs up a person to think they are bigger and better than they really are. This is what the Pharisees were doing, and Herod too, who thought his power and money were all he needed in life. None of these people had any intention at all of letting Jesus become their *Lord,* because they thought they were better than him. For him to be their Lord, they would have to serve him, and there was no way they were going to do that!

And the same goes for us. Whose strength do you really rely on each day? God's or your own? Who do you serve each day? God or yourself? Who is really your Lord? Jesus or the things and people around you who tempt you to feed your own desires and who control your life? Do you listen to Jesus, or to what the TV tells you to do? God wants to feed us with good things, like faith and hope and true love. Faith in someone who is 100% faithful to you; hope in something much more lasting than any material thing; love which will never die and is more powerful than anything in the universe. You have all these things when Jesus is your Lord. But you must humbly bow before him, giving up your stubborn pride, handing over your life into his control. You must set aside your ego and your selfish ambitions as the driving forces in your life, because they put you at the centre of your life. When Jesus is your Lord, ***he is at the centre*** guiding, healing, loving, speaking, hearing, praying, protecting. The sin of the Pharisees leaves no room for these good things. Look at the great love that goes together with Jesus' great power when he feeds the 4,000 "I feel ***sorry*** for these people, because they have been with me for three days now and have nothing to eat. If I send them away now, they will faint as they go." What a thoughtful, caring Master he is! Who ***wouldn't*** want him to be their Lord?

3. The Disciples' problem

Jesus reminds his disciples about the feeding of the 5,000 and the 4,000 people and says, "Do you still not understand?" (v. 21). He is saying in effect "Don't you understand yet that I am the ***Lord*** of heaven and earth? Why are you still worrying about little things like food for your stomach? Hasn't it sunk in yet that I can give you ***whatever*** *you* need?" It's so easy to get all worried about the practical things in life, isn't it? Now God wants us to be wise and sensible about our daily needs, like working and budgeting and being careful. But sometimes we get carried away with this. And that's what the disciples were doing. They had food on the brain, when they should have had their minds filled with spiritual things. They were really excited about all the things they were seeing, but they didn't stop to think about what it all meant. They should have been overcome with awe and trust in Jesus, instead of worrying about these other things that were little, compared to what Jesus was doing, It would be like a person in the film 'Independence Day' worrying about how many french fries he just got in his order from McDonalds when the alien spaceships arrive. When Jesus mentions yeast, the disciples think he's telling them off for not bringing along some of the leftover bread to eat. He's not talking about material things, but spiritual things which are much more important, because the spiritual thing Jesus is going to do on the cross will change the world forever.

The ultimate proof that Jesus is Lord comes when he dies on the cross for us and then he is resurrected and goes up to heaven in his body that will never die again. He is at the righthand side of God, with all power at his fingertips. He is able to help us with whatever we need. But let's not make the mistake of the Pharisees. Let's get it right Jesus is either 100% our Lord, or he's not. You either put your life 100% into his hands, or you're playing games with the most powerful man in the universe, God's Son.

Reflect and pray: God wants to bless us and look after us, but there's no such thing as a 50/50 commitment. There can only be one Lord in your life. Worship Jesus, serving him in everything you do, and you will be greatly blessed. Pray for help with those things that distract you, those things that really don't matter compared to the things of the Kingdom of God.

'See the Truth'

Read **Mark 8: 22 - 9:1**

In the previous section Jesus has been keen for people to 'see' the truth about him the truth that he is LORD. The 3 short parts in 8:22 9:1 also have something to do with seeing Jesus heals a blind man; then Peter sees the truth about who Jesus is; but then straight away Peter refuses to see the truth about Jesus' death. And in chapter 9 there is something spectacular coming that they will see with their eyes, but here in chapter 8 Jesus wants them to see something with their minds. He wants them to see who he is God's chosen Messiah who comes to save the world; and see what his real mission is to die for our sins and give us new life. This is the focal point of Mark's Gospel; he's not just telling an exciting story for entertainment, but has real purpose, to help us see who Jesus really is.

Questions: Do you see a common theme in these 3 sections?

What is so special about Jesus healing a blind person?

What is so significant about Peter's answer in v.29?

Why do you think Peter got it wrong in *v.31-33?*

Is Jesus being unfairly tough on him, calling him Satan?

Why does Jesus tell them about his death? Why might this be hard for them to accept?

When Jesus says "If any of you want to come with me you must forget yourself, and carry (or 'take up') your ......*(v.34),* what word would they have been expecting next, instead of "cross"?

What does his teaching in *v.34-38* mean for the disciples?

What does it mean for us?

When do you think the disciples would have seen "the Kingdom of God coming with power"(9: 1)?

What is stopping you from seeing Jesus and what he has achieved?

1. The Blind man sees (v.22-26)

This healing seems a bit strange, like Jesus didn't heal him completely the first time and had to try again. But this is easy to explain. The eyes were healed the first time, but all the tiny nerves and muscles hadn't been used for a long time (maybe never). It just took a bit of time for the fuzziness to clear. Jesus just put his hand over the eyes to close them and rest for a bit, then the second time the man "looked intently", exercising his eyes to bring them into focus. This is a common experience today among people whose eyesight is restored by surgery. The eyes are a very delicate part of the body. This man might also have lost a great deal of confidence in himself and was pretty shaky. Notice how Jesus "took him by the hand and led him ***out of the village",*** away from the crowd.

There are many different illnesses Jesus healed in his life on earth, but making blind people see is extra special. It's special because nobody was ever healed of blindness in the Old Testament, and because it's more than just a physical healing for the man, it's also a spiritual picture for us. When Mark writes this for us, he wants us to *see* Jesus too. In the previous story Jesus had asked some strong questions like "Don't you know or ***understand*** yet? Are your ***minds*** *so* dull? You have eyes can't you *see?"(8:17). By* healing this blind man Jesus is showing how he can make the blind see so why can't his disciples (and us) see what's really going on? Mark's Gospel is helping us to see Jesus.

There is another blind man healed in 10:46-52 and the two incidents can be seen as the brackets at each end of the central, most important section of Mark. They come just before Jesus' first prediction about his death and immediately after his third prediction about his death. The significance of his death is the most important thing Mark wants us to see.

2. Peter sees (v. 27-30)

This is the one time that Peter got it right. And if he could see who Jesus was, then the rest of the disciples could too. This is the high point of the story in terms of their understanding. Finally, they have woken up to how special Jesus is. He is the Messiah, the great King who was going to save his people and bring peace to the world, the one God had promised in the Old Testament to send. It is very important to hear Jesus' question addressed to us also. "Who do you say that I am?" We might start by answering his first question about what others think: "My minister says you are the Son of God or "My mother says you were the best man who ever lived". But it's only when you have something definite to say about Jesus for yourself, that you reveal what sort of relationship you have with him. When you can say, honestly, "He is my Lord and Saviour, my greatest friend who loves me and I love him," then you can say you know him and the blessing that flows from him.

3. Satan Stops Peter seeing (v.31-33)

It's only after Peter expresses for himself who Jesus is, that Jesus then tries to get him to understand what he's come to do. These are the 2 things we must see who *he is* and ***what he has done for us.*** Mark's Gospel up to this chapter has been focussed on who Jesus is; from here on it is focussed on what he is going to do for us. He is now consciously heading for the cross, and this is the first of three times he tells the disciples about his death. It's no good for us to just accept who Jesus is. We must also accept deeply in our hearts and minds the wonderful thing he has done for us. He died for us. This is where the life-changing power comes from, to make us completely new. This is where we see God's deep love that can save us from sin and evil and death.

It's amazing how quickly Peter can go from saying the greatest thing to the worst thing. He knows and accepts that Jesus is the Messiah, but then he just *cannot accept* what he says about his death. And it's the same with people today. Nearly everybody accepts he was a great guy, but so many will not accept that his ***dying*** is full of God's power to change people and the world. Peter wants a Messiah who will come by force a strong, powerful Messiah who will raise an army and take over Judea. He's spent a lot of time showing them his power, hasn't he? Peter doesn't want a Messiah who meekly goes to his death like a weak woman. Peter not only doesn't understand, but he violently protests "No! No Way! There's no way you can go like that!" This is the same sort of blockage to people's thinking today when they say things like "If God really cares, and Jesus is alive and powerful, then why doesn't he just come and take away all the bad things and stop all the suffering?" They won't accept God's way of fixing a damaged world through Jesus' death. Jesus says it's Satan who stops Peter and us from understanding this. Satan plays on "man's way of thinking" instead of "God's way of thinking" (v.33). Satan makes us want power through violence rather than power through love. And he makes us bang our fist on the table "I want it now!" rather than God's way of patience and faith and sacrifice.

4. The Way Jesus sees things

Sacrifice is what Jesus goes on to talk about: "If anyone wants to follow me, he must forget himself, take up his…" - his what? They would have been expecting him to say "… his *sword!"* It sounds like a call to arms. But when he said, "take up his *cross*", the smiles and cheers all around must have suddenly turned to dead silence and mouths gaping in disbelief.

They are not going to save their lives by fighting and violence, but quite the opposite; they will "lose it" because they try to save it. It's people who ***"lose their lives*** for me and for the Gospel" who will save themselves. It's people who 'go all the way' with Jesus who will truly win. Jesus' way is a way of love and self-sacrifice instead of the world's way of selfishness. It's the way of handing your whole life over to God instead of holding onto it yourself. Jesus wants us to see the powerful truth about his sacrifice and the wonderful power we can have to live the same way. Jesus' loving sacrifice is where we find real power *God's* ultimate power to change the universe. We are either ***with him*** to live and act his way, or we are "ashamed of him". His way means eternal life and happiness; the other way means death and misery, both now and "when he comes in the glory of his Father with the holy angels" that is, when he returns as judge, to end this world and start a new one of total love. We will all certainly see *that* one day - his return.

But there is one more thing Jesus wants them to see. After his death, many who are standing around him will "see the Kingdom of God come with power"(9: 1). They **will** *see* power the power of Jesus' resurrection, seeing and touching his new indestructible body. And they will also see the power of the Holy Spirit, coming into their lives to change them deeply from the inside-out. And it's the same for us. When we put our trust in Jesus we come 'face to face' with him. We see Jesus beside us every day, with the Holy Spirit powerfully living in us to change us. And when we see Christian brothers and sisters loving each other we see Jesus and his power at work.

Do you see Jesus, who he is? Do you see the truth about his death? Do you see the sort of life he wants you to live? And do you see the power of' God's Kingdom, God's Spirit working in your life? You *can* see all these things if you open your eyes and your heart to what Jesus has done for you.

Reflect and pray: For God to help us see the wonderful glory of what Jesus achieved for us on the cross. Take away any obstacles and pride, which stop us from seeing the truth. May we give up on the destructive use of power the world uses all around us, to instead seek the loving power of God that changes lives.

CHAPTER 5

Life and Death Explained

'Shine'

Read **Mark 9: 2 - 13**

This amazing experience on the mountain is like a video clip, a movie preview of what is coming later in Heaven. There's been a lot to do with 'seeing' in chapter 8, about seeing who Jesus really is. It's only after Peter has seen who Jesus is, by faith, when he said, "You are the Messiah", that Peter soon after sees the full glory of Jesus with his eyes. And it's the same for us we see by faith first, and later we will see his heavenly glory with our eyes. This is the brightest, most awesome part of Mark's Gospel, where the disciples "were so frightened they did not know what to say". It's another moment where they were filled with the fear of God, even more than when they were in the boat. There is nothing more exciting than standing in God's presence.

Questions: How did the disciples feel when they saw this shining light coming from him? Why would they feel that way?

Do you know of any incidents in the Old Testament, where something like this happened on a mountain?

Who was shining there? What sort of a light was it? Reflected?

How is this shining light with Jesus different from that Old Testament incident?

So then, what is the ***meaning of*** this incident with Jesus?

This image of Jesus shining would remain etched in the disciples' minds forever; why is it so important that there are **words** to go with it, from heaven?

Why do you think Moses and Elijah are there? What might they be saying to Jesus?

The disciples have seen so much why can't they see what he means about his death?

Who was the Elijah who had already come?

One day we will see Jesus in all his glory, just like this; how does that help our faith today?

1. Jesus Shines

What is happening here, when Jesus' clothes start "shining white whiter than anyone in the world could wash them"? Did God shine down some light from Heaven on him? No. Did his mum discover OMO? No. The closest thing to what happened here is what happened to Moses in the Old Testament. Moses went up Mt Sinai and after that he often went into the "tent of meeting", and in both these places he met with God. God came down in a cloud, and God's 'shining light' would come down on the 'Ark' the box holding the 10 commandments. When Moses came down from the mountain, or left the tent, his face would be shining, and so he put a veil over it so the people wouldn't see the 'glory' fading, which it did after a while.

All the same ingredients are in this 'meeting' with Jesus, but it's important to notice how things don't happen in quite the same way. Jesus starts shining ***before*** the cloud comes down. The shining light is not ***outside*** Jesus, making him shine too, like with Moses the light is shining out from ***inside*** Jesus. And it's not Jesus' face and hands that shine, but his clothes the glory shone out through his clothes like a veil, out from the ***centre of*** Jesus' body. What does all this mean? God's shining glory lives ***inside*** Jesus. Jesus really is God. Peter, James and John are getting a 'peek' into who Jesus really is but this time seeing God with their own eyes! What a glorious sight! This is what we will see when Jesus returns "in the **glory** of his Father, with the holy angels" as Jesus said in 8:38. How does all this help our faith today? Well, we don't see this sort of glory with our eyes, but we can be assured it is true nevertheless; these people simply could not have made up such a story. And knowing that such glory is waiting for us encourages us to keep going.

2. Elijah & Moses talk to Jesus

There was great mystery about how these two Old Testament prophets ended their lives on earth. Elijah was taken up to heaven alive, and noone knew where Moses was buried. These prophets knew the terrible pain involved when God was bringing a new stage in history with his people. Those new stages were about God setting up his ***kingdom*** with his people, like was happening with Jesus. Moses prepared the people to come into the promised land where they settled down and became a nation. And Elijah came 600 years later, after the kingdom David had set up was collapsing, and bad kings had taken over in Israel. Elijah showed them they had to trust in God as their king. Both Elijah and Moses were nearly killed by the people for the challenging words they said, and both of them were spoken to by God on Mt Sinai, where God encouraged them to trust in his power, even when things looked so dark and hopeless. Who better to send to encourage Jesus as he heads now to the terrible, dark cross? The people will want to kill him too and they will, but God's power will win the day.

God is so good to send these two to encourage Jesus. Who are the people around you who God has sent to encourage you, especially when you were facing a difficult or testing time ahead? Jesus was going to be totally deserted, all alone in his time of suffering. But he listened to these two friends from God, and he had courage to go on. You can have courage too, with some help from the friends who strengthen your faith in God.

3. The Disciples' Reaction

When the disciples saw this shining glory of God and the two prophets, they didn't know what to do or say. Peter offered to make tents, or shelters, because that's the sort of thing they did in the Old Testament when special messengers came from God. But Peter is just being distracted from what's really important, thinking he has to do something for these 'guests'. What God wants them to do is to ***look*** and be deeply impressed in their hearts and minds about who Jesus really is. So, God says to them from the cloud, "This is my own dear Son", to make it clear to them. But God doesn't only want them to look, but also to ***listen*** "listen to him!" They are to remember Jesus' words, and especially what he says about his death.

When Jesus talks to them about his "rising from death" they probably start thinking about the time when everybody will rise in the resurrection from the dead. They think this time is coming soon. But they've just seen Elijah disappear again when they thought he was supposed to come back and do some stuff before the resurrection. Jesus has to point out to them that the prophecy in the Old Testament about Elijah returning is not Elijah himself, but a prophet ***like*** him. Jesus says he has already come, and of course he's talking about John the Baptist. He points out that the Old Testament says the Messiah must suffer and be rejected, and that John has 'prepared the way' by his own suffering and death. What happened to John will happen to Jesus. The disciples must understand that this is all God's will, God's plan to save the world. They are going to be totally shocked by his death, but the things that happened on this mountain should show them that everything is on track, going ahead according to God's plan.

Reflect and pray: The physical, shining glory of Jesus is what we look forward to seeing in the end. Pray that we might make it to that end with our faith intact. Let the reality sink in, to encourage you every day.

'How <u>Much</u> Faith?'

Read **Mark 9: 14 - 29**

After the great heights of Jesus shining on the mountain, things come down to earth again with a thud. Some of the disciples had been trying to cast out a demon but failed. Why? Jesus says it was because they don't have enough faith. Mark has brought us back to the most important thing we need in our relationship with Jesus - we need faith. This is also connected to his second prediction about his death and resurrection - we only see its meaning and power by faith.

Questions: Why can't the disciples heal this boy? What might they have been thinking about, when Jesus went up the mountain with the other 3?

What should the disciples have done?

Who is Jesus angry at? Why?

How does our faith go up and down sometimes?

Why do faith and prayer go together?

What is at the centre of our faith - Jesus, or the ministers who lead us (see v.17).

What do his death & resurrection have to do with faith (v.31)?

1. Lack of faith is a real problem (v.14-19)

Jesus has been up on the mountain with Peter, James and John. The other 9 disciples had not seen Jesus shining and talking with Elijah and Moses. So in one way, their faith in Jesus might not be as strong as the other three. Also, Jesus was not with them at the time, nor were the three 'strongest' disciples, so this group of nine was a group without a leader to guide them and encourage them about what they should do. Jesus and the other three had gone off on a short excursion, and these nine probably weren't expecting to do any work while they were gone. We often find ourselves in a similar position, don't we? We're alone and get caught off guard, then something happens where we could do some good, but we don't have the confidence, we're not game enough to 'go it alone'. We know God wants us to do something, but we become scared without someone right there to show us how. What made it even harder for the nine disciples was "some teachers of the law arguing with them". These men didn't believe in Jesus at all; they were probably telling the disciples their faith was stupid. You could imagine them saying "Go on - show us how powerful your master is - heal this man - Aha! You can't! See, he's a fake, this Jesus!" This would make the disciples feel really bad, not being able to do here what they had done elsewhere when Jesus sent them out in twos (6:13). They were trying to do this faithful work with a lot of unbelief around them. They were letting all this unbelief affect them and wear them down and weaken their own faith. We often experience this too, don't we? When we're surrounded by non-believers who pay no attention to God and think our faith is silly, and maybe even make fun of us, it can be hard to stand up to them and stay confident.

But this sort of thing doesn't just affect us, but God too. Sometimes God refuses to heal someone when there is this atmosphere of unbelief. Remember when Jesus went to his hometown and he too "was not able to do any miracles there..... because the people did not have faith"(6:5-6). Jesus is just as angry this time with the disciples and the people around this man: "How unbelieving you people are!... How long do I have to put up with you?"(v.19) But Jesus is going to show them that the reason God will not give power to heal the boy is because of their lack of faith. Against the unbelief of the teachers of the Law, the crowd and the disciples, Jesus will show that his own faith in God is true.

The faith of just one person is enough to heal this boy, no matter what the odds. The father of the boy is challenged about his own faith in all this.

When he asked Jesus to help, he added "if you can", and Jesus picks up this note of unbelief, turning on him quite sharply and repeating his words back at him: "***If*** you can?"(sharper and simpler than our Good News version) Jesus then points out to him that "Everything is possible for the person who has faith". And the father answers "I do have faith.. but help me have more." This is a good answer from the father, because he has some faith, but realizes he needs more. Faith is like that - we can have a lot sometimes, and other times we have only a little. We need to keep turning to Jesus to build up our faith. Faith is really important, because it is the difference between seeing God working in our life, or not seeing God working. And our faith needs to be focused on Jesus. The man says in v.17 "I brought my son to ***you***..... but your ***disciples*** could not cast it out". This man has faith in Jesus - that's who he brought his son to see in the first place. We need to remember that our faith does not depend on God's servants, like your minister or priest. They are faulty human beings whose faith goes up and down too. No matter how badly they let you down, Jesus will never let you down. Your faith is in Jesus, not any human being.

2. The Power of Jesus can overcome anything (v.20-27)

This was a tough spirit that had been with the boy since he was very young. It had sunk its roots right into him so that it affected his whole life, trying to destroy him even by throwing him into the fire, or drowning him in water (v.22). The boy was helpless to fight it, he was under its control. Jesus has real power to free this boy, no matter how hopeless it looks to us or the disciples. To us, this boy seems to be suffering from epilepsy - simply an illness. But to everyone in the story, they are convinced it is a demon. Very often it's a case of both - a medical condition which has a spiritual side to it as well, where the demon keeps us sick. Some psychiatric illnesses can be partly caused by demons, or at least made worse, especially when the person has let the demon in through drugs or alcohol abuse, and the person becomes 'hooked'. There are lots of situations where Satan and his demons can get control over our life like this, and try to destroy us. Now it's clear that for this boy, the demon has not come into his life by giving into some addiction. But what about you? Do you feel trapped, like there is no way out from the things that are dragging your life down? Well look at what Jesus can do. He just commands the spirit that has gripped this boy, and it's gone, never to return. The evil spirit is terrified of Jesus, throwing the boy into a fit as soon as it saw Jesus, because Jesus' power is so awesome.

3. Prayer is Important (v.28-29)

Since the disciples were up against such great opposition from the Jewish teachers, from the unbelieving crowd, and from such a strong demon, they should have done a lot more serious praying. Jesus tells them this is why they failed. If their faith was strong faith in God, but was getting shaky because of what was happening around them, then they should have prayed more. Praying would have done two things: it would have given their faith more strength and confidence; and it would have given all the honour to God for the miracle. While the people were expecting these guys to heal the boy, the focus was more and more on their failure. The focus was on them. But if they had got on their knees in front of everyone and prayed, the attention and praise could only be given to God for the healing. Jesus himself doesn't do this, because the focus of attention is rightly on him - he ***is*** God. For us, we are in the situation of the disciples. We need to seriously pray to build up our faith and courage, and to honour God when we need help from him.

4. Where it's all heading (v.30-32)

After the dizzy heights of the mountain, Jesus himself brings his disciples down to earth with this second prediction of his death. They simply do not understand, and are afraid to ask him what it meant. Jesus is fixed on his goal, and only afterwards will they understand

Reflect and pray:…

'I Am the Greatest'

Read **Mark 9: 30 - 37**

The rest of chapter 9, from verse 30, is Jesus straightening out the disciples on a few key points. As he gets closer to Jerusalem in chapters 10-13, there will be many different people to deal with along the way. This end part of chapter 9 is Jesus' last chance to sit down with his disciples until the last supper in chapter14. In verses 30-37 Jesus makes two very important points about 'Who is the greatest?'

Questions: Why is it significant that Jesus ***knew*** he was going to die and rise again?

Why does he want the disciples to understand that this is the aim of his life?

What does it mean for you?

How did/does Jesus ***serve*** us?

Why does this make him the greatest?

How will serving rather than ruling make the disciples great?

How do ***you*** serve/welcome ***in Jesus' name?***

What is he saying when he takes the child and says what he does in v.37?

Does he mean that ***anyone*** who welcomes ***any*** child, welcomes Jesus?

1. 'Death Point' - Jesus' great sacrifice (v.30-32)

Jesus very much wanted his disciples to understand what his coming death and resurrection was all about. It is the most important thing for us to understand too. His death and resurrection are the whole point of him coming - it's where his real work is done. With Jesus speaking this second time now about it, there are two important things Mark wants us to understand:

1) Jesus' death is ***no mistake***. Jesus knew about it well before it happened, and it was meant to happen, it was God's plan.
2) Jesus went to his death obediently, willingly, for us. He wasn't forced by God to do it. He could have walked away at any time. His death is completely an act of love, freely sacrificing himself, for us.

It's amazing that the disciples go on to talk about who among them is the greatest, after Jesus has just been telling them ***his way*** of being the greatest. He makes the greatest sacrifice the world has ever known, and achieves the greatest victory ever known, by giving up his life and dying. This is his example for us, not to greedily hold onto life and strive for power, but to give up our lives for God's purposes, to love God and love other people.

2. 'Servant Point' - Our greatest way to live (v.33-37)

But the disciples have missed the point completely, as they argue along the way about which one of them was the greatest. These melon-headed macho males are acting like most men do when they've had a taste of power. Each one wants to be able to shout, "I am the greatest," like Mohammed Ali. But again, it is this human tendency we all have, to selfishly look at ourselves rather than other people, that gets in the way. Sin gets in the way of seeing what's really happening. This is why Jesus had to die, because there was no other way for people to be changed.

The way that Jesus wants us to be changed is for us to be able to think of others before ourselves, to be servants rather than rulers. That's what Jesus did, and it made him the greatest of all. His loving, self-giving service made him King of the universe. And that is what will make us the greatest. Jesus is saying that if we love other people in his name and give up things to serve other people and show them God's love, like Jesus did, then we will be the greatest. The more you serve, the bigger your crown will be in Heaven. So, how will you serve your Lord and people?

I remember when I used to work as a chef in a large hotel, there were various types of waiters. There were drink waiters and food waiters and the host waiter, but the 'lowest' waiter was called a 'bus-boy'. He was the one who would clear the tables and wash the dishes. He never got tips and was always bossed around. And he would regularly drop plates and get into trouble, because he had to carry large tubs of dirty dishes into the kitchen as fast as he could. It was a thankless, grotty job. Well, what sort of a servant, waiter, will you be? Jesus says, "Whoever wants to be first must place himself last of all and be the servant of all"(v,.35).

Jesus then takes it a step further. He says that even when we are facing ***children***, we are to serve them as if we were serving Jesus. Children in Jesus' day were worth nothing, and so these words were even stronger in the disciples' ears than ours. Jesus is saying that we are not only to think of ourselves as the lowest servants, but serving the lowest people too. It's like the head waiter at the Hilton turning his back on the Prime Minister in the restaurant and instead taking the lobster dinner across the road to the old wino sitting on the bench in the Fitzroy Gardens. Why does Jesus want us to serve like this? serving the lowest people? Think about it for a minute. There are two reasons:

1) He served the ***'lowest'*** people. He was already God's son in Heaven, and he ***came down*** to save us low-down sinners. To God, all of us are as low as you can get, totally lost. Just because we think we are higher than others, that's not what God thinks.
2) Every human being is ***valuable*** to God, nevertheless, and if we despise any human being just because of their age, or the way they look, or their circumstances in life, then we despise something that God has made, and his son died for. This is what Jesus means when he says, "Whoever welcomes in my name one of these children, welcomes ***me***"(v.37), because he was going to die for even the 'lowest' human being, standing in their place, as he hung on the cross.

Finally, it's important to see that when Jesus is saying to serve ***as*** the lowest servant, and serve ***to*** even the lowest people, he's not saying to serve them ***with*** any old low-down rubbish! We are to serve people with the very best that God has to offer. We have to put the words together with our actions. Jesus is not saying 'be nice to people', but to serve people "***in my name***"(v.37). We could be the best at helping people everywhere, and giving lots of money to charities, but if we were not doing it in Jesus' name, telling people about the Good News of Jesus, then we are only feeding them scraps, instead of giving them the food of eternal life and God's love. It's important in our western culture where there are lots of charities that serve lots of groups of disadvantaged or sick children, that we don't get the two confused, thinking that everybody is therefore serving or welcoming Jesus. It's only when we truly do it ***in Jesus' name*** that they have a chance of becoming God's children.

So then:

- ***Who*** do you serve? Only yourself? Only your friends?
- ***How*** do you serve? With your whole life, like Jesus did, or only with your 'leftover' time & resources?
- And ***what*** do you serve to people? Things that have little value, or the very best things God has given you, in genuine love, truth and new life?

Reflect and pray: Father of all, give me a servant heart like Jesus. Help me to see the futility of everything the world holds great, to rather know the surpassing beauty and glory of knowing you, of knowing your greater purpose for my life. Help me to see people the way you see them.

'Not a Club'

Read **Mark 9: 38 - 41**

Remember in the last study Jesus was telling his disciples how to be the greatest - by ***serving*** people like he did. The way they think of themselves is important. The greatest power is not in standing ***over*** people, but getting 'under' people, to lift them up. Jesus now talks about another common problem in the way they think about themselves. Any group of people can think of themselves as an exclusive ***club***, where the group chooses who will or will not enter the group. This is ***not*** the way for God's people. In God's group, ***God*** chooses who will come in, not us.

Questions: Why might the disciples have told this man to stop? (there is a possible good reason and a bad one).

How does the reasoning in v.39-40 work?

What do verses 39-40 have to say to us about a 'closed club' mentality that some churches fall into?

Does v.41 include any good deeds done towards any person, for any reason?

What are the key phrases in v.39 & 41? Does giving to the Red Cross or any other charity fit into either of these?

How do these verses change your focus and motivation for doing good deeds?

What is the 'reward' for a Christian?

1. "Look at what they're doing!"

The disciples are shocked that some other people who they didn't know were doing the same things as the disciples, in Jesus' name. They saw a man casting out demons, and so they told him to stop. They would have said to the man something like "Hey, you haven't been taught by Jesus, so stop using his name as if you knew him." There's a good reason why they might do this - they had respect for the name of Jesus, like they had respect for the name of God. As Jews they were brought up on the commandments, and one of them says "You shall not take the name of the Lord your God in vain." It was especially not to be used in a 'magical' way, thinking that you can make things happen by commanding God to do things for you by saying his name. This sort of thing used to happen a lot in the surrounding countries, but God told his people that they don't command him to do things, he commands them. So when the disciples see this stranger casting out demons in Jesus' name, you can understand their reaction.

Jesus points out to them that something else might be happening with this man. He says that anyone who does this sort of thing in Jesus' name will soon come to understand what Jesus is all about. Jesus is saying there is another possibility to explain why this man is doing this. It might be God who is making him do it. How are the disciples to know what God has been doing in this man's life? It might even be that this man saw what the disciples did when Jesus sent them out, and he saw and believed in Jesus through that. His understanding might be very little, but the work of God in his life might be very big.

But there is also a bad reason the disciples may have been telling this man to stop. They were jealous and bossy. They were thinking too highly of their little group, and didn't think anyone else had the right to do anything in Jesus' name. Jesus says in effect "If he's using my name, and people are being blessed through that, what right do you guys have to stop him? Don't you see that my name is all about love and blessing? If this is what's happening through this man, in my name, then he's no threat to us, but he will in fact become one of us, if you encourage him and teach him, instead of stopping him." They were thinking of themselves as a closed group of power rather than an open group of love. They need to see that God reaches out to whoever he wants, however he wants.

How do you think of the Christian group you're in? Do you think of it as a closed club? Where only those who are acceptable to you are allowed in? Look out for the ways God might be working in someone's life. Be ready to invite them in and help them understand the truth about Jesus. And don't be too worried about the strange way they might look or the strange things they might do or say. God loves each one as much as he loves you.

2. Real love is in Jesus' name

In the last verse (v.41) Jesus points out that people will also be blessed by loving us, as well as us loving them. Again, we need to be open to 'outsiders', and welcome them and love them, instead of refusing them and sending them away. When someone offers you, a Christian, something "because you belong to me", then that person does it towards Jesus. So, don't look down on someone who might be trying to help you, and try to look after those who "belong to Jesus', because they are your brothers and sisters. The people of God is not a club, but a ***family***. Jesus says any person being kind to one of his children will "receive a reward", although it's hard to understand what he means by that, if he's talking about a non-Christian showing kindness to a Christian. The key is in the words "because you belong to me", that is, they see you are a Christian, and they are therefore responding to God; God has touched them and is leading them towards his grace, and this is certainly the greatest 'reward' they could receive. If on the other hand, he's talking about a person who is becoming a Christian, or is already a Christian from another church, doing such a deed, we can understand that this person will receive their reward in heaven.

Whatever the case, the important thing to see is the words "because you belong to me", and from the earlier part "in my name". The point is that doing nice things for people is not enough. Anyone can give money to the Red Cross, or the Good Friday Appeal for the Children's Hospital, or help out a friend with some money or food, or whatever - but if they don't do it in Jesus' name then it has much less value in the long run. It's important for us to do the right things for the right reasons. If you do the right things just for your own (maybe selfish?) reasons, then there is little value in it which is true and lasting. But if you do them out of a deep love for God, out of a joyful and true relationship with Jesus who heals our insecurities and equips us for service, doing things in Jesus' name, then you honour God and he will bless you (and the other person) more and more. This is because you will be doing things to bring glory to God, rather than (as often happens) doing things to fill one's own needs.

Reflect and pray: What sort of Christian do you want to be? Just a member of a club, who's in it for what you can get out of it? Or as a truly loving person, healed and restored yourself, who wants to bless people with the love of Jesus? One way has great rewards, with the potential for ministering eternal life for others; the other is very limited, and potentially a dead end. Pray for God's grace and love to guide you in all the serving roles you are called to fulfil.

'What you do really matters'

Read **Mark 9: 42 - 50**

In the previous section Jesus talked about his people not being just a 'club'. We are not an exclusive club where we pick and choose who is in and who is out. ***God*** does the choosing and we need to be open and welcoming to new people coming in all the time.

Since Jesus expects new people to be coming into his family all the time, he now goes on to tell us about the kind of witness he expects from us. If new people are coming in, who are very 'young' in their faith, what sort of witness and example should we have towards them? Jesus says we have a very serious responsibility towards them, and we should have a good witness or else we can 'trip up' these new people and make them lose their faith. This would be a terrible thing for us to have to face God about on the Last Day.

Questions: Is Jesus saying that if your hand makes you sin, then ***go and*** cut it off?

What does he mean? Why is his language so harsh?

How do we know that sin is so serious to God?

How might we "cause a little one to stumble"? (v.42) How can we avoid this?

How are we "purified by fire"(v.49)? How are we to be like "salt"(v.50)?

Is Hell real? Why is Hell an acceptable punishment?

Does v.48 mean that punishment goes on forever? Is God cruel?

1. Stumble, trip, fall over (v.42-48)

The actual words used in each of these verses is a picture of someone tripping over something. Where it says "If anyone causes one of these little ones ***to lose his faith*** in me..."(v.42) it should say "If anyone causes one of these little ones who believes in me ***to stumble,*** it would be better...." The same is in the other verses where it says, "If your hand (or foot or eye) makes you ***lose your faith***..." it should be "If your hand makes you ***stumble***..."

It's a picture of putting something in the road so that someone falls over. So in verse 42 Jesus is talking about us doing that to someone else; if we make "one of these little ones" fall over, by putting something in their way, then we're in trouble.

What does Jesus mean**,** when he says, 'don't make them ***stumble***'? Does he mean 'don't make them ***lose their faith***, or 'don't make them ***sin'***? Our Good News Bible has chosen only one of these translations, 'lose their faith', to make it easier to read (but notice the heading - 'Temptations to ***sin'***). The word 'stumble' really means both of these things - don't make them lose their faith, and don't make them sin. And these two ideas go together, because ***how*** would you make someone lose their faith? You do that by encouraging them to sin. You do that every time your bad example leads them into sin. Jesus' words are very harsh indeed, aren't they? He's saying that if we do this terrible thing, then we might as well be dead. Imagine having a big wheel about one metre high, carved out of rock, tied around your neck, and then being thrown into the sea! It's a very hard punishment which in Jesus' day the Roman rulers often did. So it's a strong point he's making, that it's better for this to happen than for you to lead someone into sin and make them lose their faith. What sort of things do you do, that are a bad witness and could have this effect on 'young' Christians, or people of weak faith like children? Jesus wants us to change what we do, so that this doesn't happen. What we ***do*** is very important. It doesn't just affect us, but also the people around us. We need to be responsible about what we do, and take it seriously. We have power to bless people and encourage their faith in God, or we have power to destroy them by our bad example. Think about this great responsibility you have when you're doing things with your friends, your children, and even just the people in the street.

The other three verses talking about feet, hands and eyes are saying the same thing. It's better to lose an eye than to miss out on Heaven. So if your eye is the 'stumbling block' that keeps making you fall into sin, then it would be better to lose the eye and stop the sin. It would be better for you, and better for the people around you. But we need to be careful not to take Jesus the wrong way. He is not saying "If your foot makes you sin, then ***go and*** chop it off" (like a man I know, who actually did this with an electric saw). What Jesus means is "If your foot makes you sin, then ***it would be better*** to chop it off...." He's pointing out how serious it is, but he doesn't expect you to actually go and do it. He's saying that this business of leading other people into sin and losing their faith is a matter of life or Hell (v.43,45), and he doesn't want us to end up in Hell. So he puts it in the strongest way possible, to get our attention and wake us up to how important it is. He is commanding us, like the Apostle Paul does in Romans 8:13: "put to death the misdeeds of the body" and Galatians 5:16-21: "walk by the Spirit and you will not gratify the desires of the flesh… the acts of the flesh are obvious… those who live like this will not inherit the Kingdom of God."

Ultimately, we know how serious sin is when we see the extreme solution God has for it - the death of his own son. It is also important to note here that Hell is real. Jesus has no doubt about that, but the idea makes many people cringe, asking "How can a good God be so cruel?" The answer put very briefly is that God can do what he likes, and the seriousness with which he regards our actions is in line with the very high dignity with which he has made us "in his image", to be "like him" (see Genesis 2). The high level of dignity and responsibility he has made us with means a high level of accountability which he cannot ignore. The huge dignity and tragedy of our situation as sinners is also in line with the huge solution and sacrifice God comes up with in his own son's death for us. Hell is not too harsh a judgement for humans to pay, just as his own son's death is not too large a price for God to pay.

We should also get the point of v.48 correct. The point is not that punishment in hell goes on forever, but that it ends in destruction. Fire and worms in the Bible punish for a short time, and then destroy completely. It's the ***instruments*** of destruction that remain forever as a sign of God's justice, not the punishment, which ***would*** make God cruel if it were so. This language comes directly from the last verses in Isaiah (and the disciples would have recognized this reference), where the purpose is to encourage the faithful in persevering with difficulties because God's judgement in the end will be complete, vindicating the faithful and destroying forever everything and everyone who is full of sin and evil.

2. Lots of Salt! (v.49-50)

Finally, Jesus uses a more positive picture to encourage us in the same thing. We are supposed to be like salt, with plenty of sharp taste. When people see us, they should see a strong witness. And like salt is used to preserve things, we should be doing things that preserve lives, not destroy them. We're supposed to stand out, not blend into the rest of the world and its sin, and become bland and tasteless. The picture of fire and salt in v.49 means the same thing, that our witness, even through 'fiery trials' of temptation or persecution or even illness, will be for our good and the good of others;

the idea of our lives being purified by 'fire' is a common New Testament theme (see 1Peter 1:6-7). We are supposed to do good - the greatest good - by having a good witness that doesn't give into sin but fights against it. So like salt kills germs in food, 'be salty', so that you kill sin in your life and you become an agent that preserves life in others, a faithful person in your witness to others.

Reflect and pray:...

'One True love, for Life'

Read **Mark 10: 1 - 12**

Jesus is not afraid to talk about the hard things in life, as we have seen in chapter 9. But this part of his teaching in ch.10 is without doubt the hardest thing for us to accept today. The idea of just one husband or wife for life is a nice and wonderful thing, we say, so long as we stay ***happy*** together. But what really happens for 99% of couples is that marriage is hard work. It's not all a 'bed of roses', like our world expects it to be, like we see on TV. Our world tells us "When things get tough, get out." But Jesus says this is very wrong. This is not God's way for us, and it is not what's really good for us. God made us to have one sexual partner, for life. How boring! But Jesus didn't back away from this hard teaching, and neither should we. We should really listen to it, because it is strong medicine for our sick, emotionally confused world.

Questions: Do you consider this to be one of the hardest teachings of Jesus? Why?

What is the abuse of the Pharisees which Jesus is addressing?

How were women regarded in Jesus' day?

Do you think Jesus follows that line, or does he even things up for women? How? What was the result of a woman being divorced in those days, financially for herself and children?

The Pharisees had made divorce an easy thing to do - is this like our society today? Is this what God wants?

Why is divorce so damaging to families; what are the effects?

Does this mean God is ***never*** in favour of a particular divorce?

Does this mean a divorced person can ***never*** remarry?

Does God expect our relationships to be perfect?

What can we do when things go wrong?

Can things ever get so bad that God can't forgive us and won't help us to get back on our feet, to live the good way he wants?

Is there enough power in Jesus' death and resurrection to change even our sexual habits and weaknesses?

1. Jesus evens things up for women.

In Jesus' day, women had a lot stacked against them, and they were really treated as things rather than people, as something to be bought and sold (and the media still does this sort of thing today). Even the most religious people found a way to abuse women and make this seem like an OK thing to do. There was just one little verse in Deuteronomy 24, where Moses allowed a man to divorce his wife, if he found "some indecency" in her, and there were 2 ways you could understand this. It could mean something very serious, like your wife committing adultery (and this is the proper way to understand it), or you could use any little thing to just get rid of your wife - she might burn dinner, or not look nice, or put on weight. So this is why the religious leaders ask Jesus this question "to trick him", because they knew that some people in the crowd would disagree with him, no matter which way he answered.

Jesus answered the hard way, the right way, which went against the popular way of thinking. He pointed out that Moses wrote this verse only because people have such hard hearts. God's plan from the beginning was not for marriages to break up. The much bigger law of God is found in Genesis chapters 1 and 2, where husband and wife "become one" and should never be separated. This is what God really wants, instead of selfish, irresponsible husbands trying to find an easy way out so they can go onto the next young bird that takes their fancy. No man has the right to treat a wife this way, and it's right there in God's law, that husband and wife are equal partners who become one. But the way the Law is stated in other books of the Old Testament like Exodus and Deuteronomy, in very male terms, things seem to be greatly stacked against women. A man could divorce a woman, but a woman could not divorce a man on any grounds. What Jesus points out is that in fact the rules are ***the same*** for both man and wife. What men were doing, using the law as an excuse to do what they like and leave their wife destitute, wiping their hands of responsibility and commitment, is completely unacceptable to God and Jesus.

2. Divorce is hard, not easy

Jesus wants us to realise that marriage and relationships are very important stuff to God and very powerful stuff in our lives. Sex is not to be taken lightly, as just a 'fun thing', to jump in and out of whenever we like. When two people come together like this, it is the most life-changing thing they can ever experience. They will never be the same again. It is so special and so powerful, where one person gives their life, their very essence, to another person. For them to separate is a most unnatural and traumatic thing.

Some people think you can just go in and out of sexual relationships at will, and it doesn't really matter; the aim is to stay happy. Sometimes they don't realise the trail of pain and destruction they leave behind them. Sometimes they just don't care. Sometimes they do hurt very deeply themselves and they push it down, try to ignore it, and stay busy with new things to distract them from the pain. Whatever the case, the danger is we become either hard in our hearts, so that we use people, or we become so hurt and dependent on people that they use us. We end up wasting the good and special thing God has given us, and never really find the happiness that we so much seek and need. "Breaking up is hard to do", as the song says, because it goes violently against the way we are made, it damages us. And so it goes against God too, because he's the one who has so beautifully made us.

Don't let anyone make you believe it's easy to break up, because it's not - it's very hard indeed. My wife Kerry and I have been through some very rough times in our marriage, and even to the point of thinking it was all over. All the way through, it has been my wants and desires which have brought about the greatest tension. Very often people get sucked into the way the world expects us to be in our relationships, in it for what we can get out of it. The power of the media, which tries to get us to always want something better, instead of cherishing and enjoying the good things we have - this power is immense, but very subtle and influencing, if we let it. I thank God that he has kept Kerry and me together by helping us work through issues which have come up, so that we can be truly happy. It has been very hard sometimes, but I certainly appreciate the wonderful wife God has given me.

3. So, what are we supposed to do?

- Take marriage (and sex) very seriously (Once you're 'united' in a sexual relationship, you ***are*** married as far as the Bible is concerned). It is the greatest enjoyment a human can experience, but it is also the most powerful. The fire can fuel your happiness, or it can burn you badly.
- Don't enter a relationship just for sex - love is much more than that. A relationship based on sex is like a chair with only one leg - it won't 'stay up' for very long. It needs the other legs of friendship, commitment and understanding. These things make for ***unselfish*** love, ***true*** love, ***stable*** and life-***giving*** love like our Lord Jesus has shown us. This is what will make us truly happy.
- Choose ***wisely*** who you marry - really get to know them well, patiently, and leave the sex part until last, which is the right way around, the 'icing on the cake', not the foundation for a great relationship.

- If things get tough, then ***work*** at it, no matter what it takes, because anything this good is worth fighting for, not giving up on.
- If after all the work, things are so bad you're about to kill each other, then it's better to divorce. Divorce is the absolute last option, and is allowed by God in extreme circumstances - this is why God has made this allowance in the Law of Moses. God knows that our frail sinfulness can be so stubborn to change, that it's better to take the lesser of two evils than to be at war with each other.
- Think very, very seriously about any remarriage (including a sexual relationship), as this is the greater sin in Jesus' eyes. And if the urge for divorce and remarriage (or defacto relationship) comes from romantic feelings for someone else, then this is the very worst scenario. This is what Jesus denounces so strongly with the Pharisees, the very thing they were doing. This is where you have to sort out your true motives, and maybe even your reasons for living, your whole purpose in life.
- Most importantly, even if your relationship(s) do get into a terrible mess, remember that Jesus' death forgives every sin, and he has a way out for you, no matter how bad things have become. "If we confess our sin, he will keep his promise and.... will forgive us"(1 John 1:9). We are never beyond God's mighty power to save us, if we really want him to, if we truly repent and turn to him for help. (And remember, repentance is more than just saying you're sorry - it means a total change of direction, as we saw in ch.1).
- Finally, realise that God's great love through his Son can give us power to control our passions, instead of our passions controlling us. And he can give us healing for past hurts, contentment instead

of frustration and anger, understanding and peace instead of confusion, and real freedom to be happy instead of being driven by our desires and the expectations of other people - free to be the lovely and loving person he made you to be.

4. A further thought for today

In our time, where the LGBTQ lobby has confused many, it is worth considering Jesus' answer to the question in Mark in another way. A tricky question these days would be: "Is it okay for same sex attracted people to marry each other?" If Jesus was asked that question today, I reckon he would answer with exactly the same words he did back then. Try reading his answer again, but in this modern context.

Reflect and pray:...

'The Upside-down Kingdom'

Read **Mark 10: 13 - 31**

Do you see how these 2 stories go together? The last verse could almost go with the first story, because the "last of all" in Jesus' day were ***children***. They were thought of as things, really, rather than people. Jesus is giving us one of his most important teachings, that the way we see things is not the way God sees them. In the Kingdom of God, things are turned upside-down - the rich people become poor, and the poor become rich; the big become little and the little people become big. How do ***you*** see people - the way God does, or the way the world does?

Questions: Why did Jesus confront this man like he did?

Why did Jesus make such an outrageous demand?

What is the simple point common to both of these stories?

Does "receive the Kingdom like a child" mean 'be childish'? What does it mean?

Should we all go sell everything we have and give to the poor, to enter the kingdom?

In what ways might we be confronted with things God wants us to give up, in order to enter the Kingdom?

Why would God want us to give them up?

What sorts of things do people keep as a 'reserve' god, these days?

How far are we prepared to go in trusting Jesus, if he asks us to?

What is God challenging you to give up? How can you do it?

1. Little Children - be like them

Jesus points to little children as an example of what ***we*** should be like, if we want to be in God's Kingdom. He isn't saying we should be immature and silly, like children can be, but we should be ***trusting*** like children are, and depend on God, like children depend on parents for everything. As adults we like to depend on ourselves, or things like money, or even other people, instead of depending on God, trusting in him. Young children have a simple trust in the people who are ***really good for them***, the people who care for them and love them. We need to wake up that God is like this towards ***us***, if we just trust in him.

We need to realise that trying to be big in the way the world tries to be big, is not good for us. What is really good for us is to come to Jesus, for him to bless us, like he did with these children. The disciples think they are big and important, and so they shoo away the children, thinking they shouldn't waste Jesus' time. But the children are just as important to Jesus, and they are in fact much better in their attitude to Jesus than the disciples are. So how do you think about yourself? Do you think you are only little, and so you fight to be big? That's not the way God sees you - all he wants is for you to come to Jesus for him to bless you - then you will be really big - you will be God's child in God's Kingdom, forever. Jesus doesn't beat us over the head to make us his children, but he gently ***calls us*** to ***come to him***. You can either come to him like a child, realising that he has everything that is really good in life to give, or you can keep striving to get everything the world tells you is good, like depending on yourself, and having everything you want right now - but all of this will only destroy you, and make you ***un***happy, really. Be like a child and have the good sense to go to the person you can really ***trust*** and is ***really good*** for you and can give you everything your heart desires - Jesus.

2. Little Riches - don't like them too much

Jesus knows what is going on inside this man's heart. This man ***does*** want to be part of God's Kingdom. He tries very hard to do all the right things and be a good person. He seems quite genuine about all this; notice how Jesus "looked at him with love"(v.21). He thinks he is able to do all the good things God requires and get into God's Kingdom. Jesus however shows him that there is something missing. This man wants to hold onto his riches ***and*** God, and Jesus says this is impossible.

This man is an example for all of us, too. Very often we try to hold onto something else as a second god in our lives, a sort of 'reserve' god, like an insurance policy. We say "Yes, I love Jesus, and depend on him, but I also need this other thing to keep going." When we do that, we show how we don't really depend completely on Jesus. Jesus is able to look after all things, at all times, and God is not impressed when we abuse his love for us by turning to something else. He is not talking about other good things like doctors and medication and good friends to talk to, or even money in and of itself - he's talking about 'addictions of love' to things which have become unhealthy blockages in our relationship with God, and stop us from loving people the way God loves people. If this young man loved people the way God does, he would have a heart of compassion for the poor and want to help them by giving his money away like Jesus said. But he has an addiction to his money, he loves it too much and he is not prepared to go through the pain of giving it up.

What is your addiction? Is it money, or sex, or some sort of drug like alcohol or cigarettes, or living in a social media fantasyland, or telling lies so that people accept you? Some people even make a god out of their family. There are lots of things that try to compete with God in our world today. They are attractive, they are the easy way, whereas it is in fact "hard" to enter the Kingdom of God (v.23, 24, 25). These things strongly influence us, if we let them. But Jesus has the power to set us free from them. Sure, it might be painful to give them up, initially, but we will be much happier in the end, living on the truly good things Jesus has to give us, the things of God's Kingdom, like true love, peace of mind, good friends, feeling good about ourselves, better physical health, and ***freedom*** from the powers of the world that try to control us and drag us down. The rich young man doesn't think he can live if he is set free from his love of money, but he is wrong; his life would be much, much happier. He is being controlled by the evil power that says money is happiness.

Is Jesus saying that we should give away all of our money, to get into the Kingdom? Or walk away from our family and other responsibilities? No, he isn't. What he's saying is if money - or some other thing - is ***stopping us*** from entering God's Kingdom, stopping us from handing our lives over into God's hands, then we need to 'give it up', in one way or another. No amount of 'doing good things', like this man did, will make up for material greed, and get us into the Kingdom of God. God doesn't want our good deeds, ***he wants our whole life*** - so he can bless us, to receive "a hundred times more"(v.30), and change us into something lovely, something like his Son Jesus. He wants us to truly know his love and be able to truly love others like he does, with a powerful, pure love which is the most valuable thing in the world. So don't let your love of something else stop you from experiencing God's love and living God's love. This is what all the Old Testament laws are really about, as Jesus points out for this young man - they are all about loving God and loving each other. As we follow God's good laws, we need to do them ***from a heart of love***, rather than just thinking of our own reputation or even our own salvation, like this man was.

Reflect and pray: These last 2 studies have focused on sex and money – the two most compromising, corrupting elements in human life. Nothing has changed in 2,000 years! Pray that the Lord of love will intervene when you are tempted by these things. Left alone, we are vulnerable, but when we reach out, ready to be guided and protected, it is amazing the ways God always comes through, diverting us from disastrous consequences.

'Now I see Jesus'

Read **Mark 10: 46 - 52**

This meeting with blind Bartimaeus is another one of those 'turning - points' in the Gospel story, and as mentioned earlier, this miracle of sight acts as 'brackets' with the one in 8:22-26, with the three predictions about Jesus' death in between. The central point in Mark's message is for us to ***see*** the truth about Jesus' death and resurrection.

This is the end of Jesus' wandering ministry. There is only the cross ahead now, and his final preparation for that. This is his last miracle with a person, and the one he wants us to keep in our minds always, because it is a picture of our spiritual walk with Jesus. All of us are blind at some time, and we don't see Jesus. We can only see Jesus through faith. In this story there are 2 stories running at the same time - the story of the man Bart and his 'blind faith', and our story of discipleship, how ***we*** see Jesus by faith.

All through Mark's Gospel, he has been wanting us to get to know the real Jesus. The way we get to know him is not just by knowing ***about*** him, but by ***'seeing'*** him, seeing who he really is. In ch.9 especially, there were lots of things to do with seeing: 3 disciples who saw his shining glory on the mountain; there were demons who saw who he really was; and Jesus tried to make his disciples see his way of winning the fight by dying, and being the greatest by serving. The disciples, the crowds, and the religious leaders had all failed to see him for who he really is, and now this blind Bart, a poor and simple man, is the final great example of someone who ***sees*** Jesus, by faith.

Questions: How did Bart know about Jesus? Why did he call out to Jesus? What does "Son of David" show that he knows about Jesus?

What does Bart mean when he says, "Have ***mercy*** on me"?

Do we need God's mercy? Why?

Why is this healing so significant?

How are the steps in Bart's experience a pattern for us to follow?

What is faith? Why does Jesus say, "Your ***faith*** has healed/saved you"?

Why does faith work, whereas knowledge, understanding, cleverness & 'doing the right thing' don't work?

1. The Man - 'Blind Faith'

The people in Jericho tried to shoo away Bart just like the disciples tried to shoo away the children earlier in this chapter. It was an exciting festival time, and Jericho was like a gateway to Jerusalem for the Passover. It was an important stop-over because it was 15 miles from Jerusalem. This was the distance set down in the Law, where people living within 15 miles all around Jerusalem had to come to the Passover. Anyone living further away didn't have to come. So the ones who did come through Jericho, on their way to Jerusalem, were only the most dedicated ones, and often the wise teachers who had come from a long way away. These 'travelling preachers' were the ones the people especially wanted to hear as they came through. And so the people were excited that this famous Jesus might have some wonderful teaching to share, and Bart's shouting was an annoying distraction.

By what he was calling out, however, this blind Bart showed a deep understanding about who Jesus was. He could 'see' something from what he had ***heard*** about Jesus, and this came out in two things he said: First, he called out to Jesus as "Son of David". Bart knows that Jesus is the Messiah, the new King David who the Bible promised would come. He knows that this Son of David was bringing the blessings of Heaven. And so he knew that Jesus could cure his blindness, even though he had ***never seen*** Jesus do a miracle but only heard about it. Second, he called out "Have mercy on me". What does he mean when he says "Have ***mercy*** on me"? Does he mean 'Take ***pity*** on me', like in our Good News translation? or 'be ***kind*** to me', or '***forgive*** me', or '***help*** me', or what? It means all of these things rolled together. It amounts to "Please, give me my life back". He knows that he is totally helpless to change things himself, and only God in his kindness can give him back his sight, even though he doesn't deserve it. And he knows this can come through Jesus.

The Meaning - Our Faith

We need to understand that all of us are just like Bart. We are blind, we are in the dark, and we need Jesus to give us our life back. All of us need God's ***mercy*** that comes through Jesus. There is a pattern for us to follow in this story with Bart:

- We ***are lost***, in darkness, hopelessly suffering with no good future.
- We must look at ourselves and wake up to the fact that ***we need*** God to save us.
- We can cry out to Jesus for ***mercy***, and ***keep crying out*** until he answers.
- We will 'see' Jesus, by ***faith.***

- If we have truly been saved by him, then we will ***follow*** Jesus for the rest of our life.

These are the things that happen with Bart, and it's Jesus giving his last 'miracle-message' to the people. This is the all-important message of Mark's Gospel. When Jesus says to Bart "Your faith has ***healed*** you", the word he uses for 'healed' is also the word for 'saved', and should really be translated "Your faith has ***saved*** you", because Bart is not only healed physically, but also spiritually, as he puts his trust for the whole of his life into Jesus' hands. This is why he goes on to follow Jesus, because his ***whole life*** has been saved, not just his eyes.

But what is faith?

If we're expected to follow Bart's example of faith, then we should maybe answer the question "what ***is*** faith?" Bart helps us to see that faith is completely ***trusting*** in Jesus. But where does it come from? How do you 'turn it on?'

Faith is not just saying to yourself "I believe, I believe", trying to hypnotise yourself and make yourself believe something. Faith is not something inside you that you 'turn on'; it's something that you either have or you don't have. Where does it come from? It's something that God gives us, where he gently opens our eyes and our hearts to see him. And then once we ***have*** it, we need to ***use*** it, we need to exercise it and let it grow. So it's not something we use to work our way to God, but it's a special gift from God where we give up on doing things ourselves and simply trust in God. Bart ***had*** this thing called faith, and then he wasn't afraid to ***use it***, to keep calling out to Jesus.

Reflect and pray:...

Life on the Line: final arguments with the authorities

'The End Begins'

Read **Mark 11: 1 - 11**

This is the beginning of the end for Jesus, the last stage in his earthly life. If we were watching a movie, this would be Part 3, where we see the final, terrible end of a hero. Jesus is entering Jerusalem for the last time. He is walking into a trap, and he knows it. This is the point of no return, and it's like a grey-red cloud comes over the scene from here through to the end.

When Jesus enters Jerusalem 3 things happen: Jesus picks up his transport (the donkey), the people celebrate as he enters the gates, and then he does a bit of sightseeing in the temple. It all seems a bit simple and straightforward, really, something kids have fun with, in a school pageant with dress-ups and palm branches. But it is nothing quite so childish. Rather, it's another one of those very serious, dramatic 'turning-points' in Jesus' life. What we really have is: 1) The King of the universe rides in just as the prophets said he would; 2) The people welcome this king; and 3) the King surveys his throne-room.

Questions: The first 7 verses are about the disciples ***getting*** the donkey, and there are only 4 verses about his entry into Jerusalem after that. Why? What is the point of this?

What sort of a king would enter like this?

Why are the people doing & saying the things in v.8-10?

How much awareness did they really have about who Jesus was and his mission?

What do you think Jesus might be thinking about as he looks around in the temple? How might he feel at this time?

How does God win victory over sin & evil? How do we?

1. The King Rides in

The King doesn't come riding in on a big white horse to save his princess bride from the black knight, like in the fairytales. This is in fact the sort of thing he ***will*** achieve in the end, even though it doesn't look like it here, and it will be powerful and ***real***, not just fantasy. Jesus is coming in disguise by riding on this donkey. It's a disguise for those who don't know what's going on. But some would have understood that the Messiah, the King they were waiting for, was supposed to come exactly like this. It's a ***humble*** way in, that gets past the Roman guards' attention and lets Jesus slip into

Jerusalem almost unnoticed, because this is the way lots of people were welcomed to the festival. It's a great time of celebration and gathering in the city. Jesus doesn't want to be speared at the gates for starting a riot. There is a much more deliberate plan for his death - a step-by-step plan with signs along the way for people later to understand who he was and what he was doing. His death was no accident, but according to God's plan.

This planning is so obvious when Jesus sends his disciples to get the young colt. It all seems so mysterious, as Mark spends 7 verses telling us about getting the animal, and only 4 verses telling us about what happened after that. Why does Mark tell it in such detail? Because we are supposed to get a sense of how God is directing everything. And it was supposed to be a sign, showing what he was up to, to give a hint that this was all part of God's plan. Jesus has most likely been planning this for a long time; he probably arranged everything with the owners on a previous visit, telling them he would be up for Passover, and he would send his disciples to fetch it, with the password "The Lord needs it now". But there is also the chance that there is even more of God's direction in this, where maybe Jesus and the owners have never met, and a dream or a vision from God has guided them. This fits well with the mysterious way Mark tells the story. Either way, Jesus' plans are in line with God's plans, and people are supposed to see that Jesus was coming as God had said he would in Zechariah 9:9, riding on a donkey.

2. The People Welcome this King

The people are just caught up in the usual frenzy of the festival, lining the streets like we do in Melbourne for Moomba or in Sydney for the Mardi Gras. Sure, there are extra police for the event, but there's nothing unusual when Jesus is greeted like this. He's just another Jewish teacher, and yes, they were hoping one of them would be the Messiah. But ho-hum, that's what happened at this time of year, and the Roman authorities had seen it all before - just high hopes and people having a party. The difference in Jesus' case was ***the Jews*** and their attitude. Jesus was attracting too much attention for their liking, since they didn't approve of him. They were the ones who had an inkling of what he was claiming to be, and so Jesus was putting himself in a very dangerous position, entering Jerusalem so openly like this.

What the people were singing and doing was ironically perfect for welcoming this great king, even if they didn't understand at all what was about to happen. Laying cloaks on the ground was a usual way to welcome a king (see 2 Kings 9:12-13), and waving the branches was the way to celebrate the Passover. Passover was the time Israel remembered the great saving of their people from Egypt, and here Jesus was coming to save the people again. When they sing "Hosanna", this means 'save us', or 'save now'(not quite 'Praise God' as we have in this version). This had become a victory song for the people who hoped for the day they would be free from the Roman Empire. All the things the people expected, about freedom coming and salvation coming, were indeed happening in Jesus. But the ***way*** it was going to happen, by him dying and bringing ***spiritual*** freedom, was not at all what they expected or wanted. This powerful, new salvation was hidden from their eyes at this stage, and even hidden from the disciples until after Jesus was raised from the dead and the Holy Spirit came.

3. The King surveys his throne-room

This is a spine-tingling moment for Jesus. He is the King, coming into his temple, the place where God had set up his throne as King of the world. Here he is, looking upon it quietly, thinking about this place being destroyed forever. It is a deep moment for Jesus, who had the right to claim this place as his own, and take control of it - and he could have - and yet he doesn't. There is a much more powerful way that God has designed for him, a way that would see him seated on a heavenly throne, with absolute power over all the universe, to save people forever while also becoming the judge of the world. But this would only happen the other side of death - death God's way, on a cross, in pain and humility and shame. The King who came quietly and humbly to his death, on a donkey, will indeed return on a powerful white horse to gather his people and to judge the world (see Revelation 19:11-16).

There are two things for us to think about when we read this:

1. We should ***worship*** Jesus for his great courage and love. He obediently followed his Father's plan, to save us. Thank him and praise him and let him be your Lord and hero. Don't be like the crowd, who were excited about getting together for a party, but didn't ***see what God was doing.*** These great things have happened for our lives to change, not just to have fun. Open your eyes to see what God is doing in your life now.
2. Follow Jesus' example of peace and love, as the way to overcome evil. He didn't come with violence, but with love and sacrifice. And if we keep in mind that Jesus will return one day to take us with him, this should encourage us to hold true to the one who really loves us, no matter how hard things get for us in this life.

Reflect and pray: Take the time to sit and ponder the huge implications of this scene. Picture the events. Get a sense of the gravity of the situation. Praise and thank your Lord and Saviour, for his unmatched courage, faithfulness and love, to plan his own death, for you. Pray for courage and God's grace, to follow his example.

'Action Stations'

Read **Mark 11: 12 - 26**

Jesus has come into Jerusalem for the last time, and now he stirs things up in a big way. Some would say he's gone mad, but no, it's all part of the plan. In this story there are 3 things: 1) the fig tree is a sign for us to see the meaning of what he's doing, 2) there's the action where he does things a prophet does, in the temple and 3) his explanation to the disciples, trying to get them to think about the important thing he's showing them.

Questions: What's going on with this fig tree - why does Jesus get upset when there's no fruit and it isn't the season for fruit? What is he doing?

Why does he do such an aggressive thing in the temple?

Won't this attract the wrong sort of attention? Is he suicidal?

Is it OK for him to be so angry? Why?

Is it OK for us to get angry like this?

What do you make of his answer to Peter about the fig tree?

Why doesn't he tell Peter the ***meaning*** of the fig tree?

Can we pray for absolutely anything and expect to get it?

1. The Fig tree - a sign (v.12-14 & 20)

The fig tree and the grape vine were common pictures of Israel in the Old Testament. When Jesus 'talks' to the fig tree, it's a symbol of him talking to Israel, or in particular talking to Jerusalem, or even more particularly the temple in Jerusalem. This city and this temple were at the centre of Israel's life as God's people. When Jesus gets upset at finding no fruit on the tree, even though it's covered with leaves, we can get the impression that he's just throwing a temper tantrum because he wanted some figs. But that's not it; he doesn't call down God's curse on the tree out of temper, but as a sign for the disciples. He knows that it's not the right season for figs, but when he goes to the tree, all lovely and green with leaves but no fruit, that's what Israel is like - all show and no 'fruit', no food for the people. They were supposed to be the feeders of their country and the world around them - not with normal food but with the spiritual food of God's word, the spiritual food of God's plan to save the world. In another way, they were supposed to show the 'fruit' of true worship and praise and trust in God so they would see the 'fruit' of new people coming to know God. Sadly, this was not happening, and that's what made Jesus angry.

So when Jesus does this amazing miracle that destroys the tree in 12 hours with just a word, it's a sign of God's judgement on Israel. Since they do not have the 'fruit of faith', since they are 'out of season', out of tune with God's timing, and not ready to meet their Messiah, their King, they will kill him, and 70 years later their precious temple will be destroyed, never to be built again. (I have been to Israel and seen the massive imprint of the temple, the flat expanse of the foundations; it was an awesome experience, recognizing that it's been like this for nearly 2,000 years).

2. The action - of a prophet (v.15-18)

What Jesus saw happening in the temple really showed what was happening in the hard hearts of Israel's leaders. They were interested in getting money to rebuild their beautiful temple, rather than serving their people and worshipping God the way they should. They had turned God's place of prayer into a marketplace, and even sometimes cheating people out of their money. When Jesus starts turning over tables and chasing people out, he is doing two things: 1) He is truly angry at what he sees and so he does what is right in his heart and right in God's eyes to do; there is such a thing as righteous anger, and Jesus is no pussycat, he is expressing God's anger at something which is clearly wrong; 2) Even more significantly, he is now acting like a prophet. He is stirring things up so they will know he is a prophet and the result of this will be that they will kill him. This is exactly what happens to many prophets in the Old Testament when they start challenging the leaders about what they are doing wrong. God always put his prophets above the leaders of Israel; the leaders were supposed to listen to them. But instead, they often just killed them to get them out of the way, to keep their power and keep doing what was wrong. Jesus is making sure that everyone understands he is a prophet. They are not just going to kill some carpenter's son, or even a wandering preacher, but the great prophet they had all been waiting for (see Deuteronomy 18:15-18, and Acts 3:22).

Is Jesus mad? Is he like some poor, suicidal people who in recent years have waved a knife at police, and then been shot dead? That's how dangerous this act of Jesus' is. Or is he the bravest person that ever lived, knowingly sacrificing himself to save the world from sin and God's judgement? We need to realise that this was God's way, the only way, to save us. We need to realise that it's not just the Jews and the Roman emperor who kill Jesus, but we are ***all*** responsible for Jesus' death, because of our sins.

3. Jesus explains - about prayer (v.22-25)

It's interesting how Jesus doesn't explain about the fig tree to his disciples like I have explained it at point 1. We're supposed to see all those things for ourselves, like the disciples saw it and later came to understand it, and like Mark does when he's telling the story. But when Jesus himself explains his curse on the fig tree to the disciples, he homes in on the main point - pray with real faith. That's what he didn't find in the temple, and that's what will make all the difference in their understanding of Jesus. Jesus is showing them what true religion is all about. It's not about doing ceremonies in a pretty building, but it's about seeing what God is doing, trusting in him, opening your life up to him and letting him change your life. None of us can change our own life by the things we do - in little ways we might, but not in the big important things like peace with God and overcoming sin in our life. These things can only be changed by God, as we put our faith in God and pray to him from the heart.

So Jesus says to the disciples in effect "Are you impressed by what I did to the fig tree? This is a very little thing. Much bigger things than this can be done with faith and prayer, and what's more, ***you*** can do it!" Now it's important to understand that when Jesus says "Whoever tells this hill to get up and throw itself in the sea.... it will be done for him.... you will receive whatever you ask for", Jesus is not expecting us to be asking for crazy things. He's giving a crazy example to show how nothing is beyond God's control, but he's expecting that we will be asking for the things ***God wants***, if we're praying in faith. So if, after faithful prayer the Holy Spirit made it clear to you that God had a ***reason*** for wanting a hill to be thrown in the sea, then he would certainly do it if you ask. But God won't answer prayers the way we want if we're just showing off or being greedy - "God let me win Tattslotto" prayers. God also won't answer revenge prayers -

"God kill that person who's bugging me", because if God has forgiven ***us*** rotten sinners, then how can we be unloving and unforgiving to the people around us (v.25)?

How can we sum up this part of Mark's Gospel? Well, Jesus is not just a prophet who storms in, wrecks the place and then goes off by himself in a huff. No, he stays with his disciples on the way to the cross, no matter how frustrating and painful that might be. He works hard, teaching them with words and signs, to get them to ***understand*** that he's the great prophet from God, who is changing God's true religion forever, so that people will worship God in faith and prayer ***everywhere***, not just in the temple at Jerusalem.

Reflect and pray: 'Lord Jesus, full of grace and power, come into my life as King. Help me to see you for who you really are. Help me to understand your purposes for my life, and how you would have me act in your world. Grant me wisdom to know how to pray and how to listen, with your priorities reigning in my life, instead of all the meaningless distractions around me.'

'Battle of Wits - Part I: The Challenge'

Read **Mark 11: 27 - 12:12**

This question to Jesus from the priests and teachers starts a new part in the drama leading up to the cross. Earlier, we have seen two visits to the temple: in verse11, we have had the quiet, scary scene in the temple, with Jesus looking around - the calm before the storm; then we have had the stormy trashing of the temple; and now on his third visit we have the battle of wits - the questions and answers. This part is like a police inquest, before they decide whether to lay charges or not against Jesus. Or it's even more like a Town Hall meeting, where the town leaders are trying to get to the bottom of what's creating all the stir in town. That's what the outer courts of the temple were like - a place for town meetings, with lots of people around. When these religious leaders approach Jesus it would have attracted a lot of attention. They are out to disgrace Jesus and have him thrown out, because the sort of things he was doing were just not allowed in their respectable town. But this 'town hall meeting' goes on for longer than they expect. It doesn't end until the end of chapter 12, and by that time the leaders have been silenced by Jesus' responses, and he is free to turn the attack on them, showing them up for the phonies they really are. By the end of this public hearing the officials know they are never going to get Jesus legally, and so their plot to kill him takes a much more sinister, unlawful turn after this.

Questions: Where ***does*** Jesus' authority come from? Do the religious leaders know this? How?

What sort of answer would they have been expecting from Jesus?

Do the people around them know where Jesus' authority came from?

Why doesn't Jesus give a straight answer, but turns the tables on them with a question of his own?

What sort of Old Testament role is Jesus playing here, and how is that connected to John the Baptist?

Explain the different parts of the parable, in terms of God's 'big story' with his people.

How wise is Jesus, and how aware is he of the 'big picture' of what God is doing through him?

How does this help us today?

1. The Challenge

Jesus comes to the temple for the third day now, with his disciples, and he is confronted with a group of religious leaders coming toward him. And they are not just ***one*** of the religious groups in Jerusalem, but all three of them - the priests, the teachers of the Law, and the elders. This in itself was an unusual sight, seeing these 3 groups banding together, because they tended to have disagreements with each other. All three groups had a common enemy in Jesus, and coming together against him like this would have attracted a lot of attention.

The first question they ask him is in relation to what happened the day before, when he cleared out the temple. They ask "By what authority do you do these things? Who gave you the right to upset things in our temple?" The way Jesus answers is very unexpected. He talks about John the Baptist, and he answers their question with a question about him. Jesus knows how important John was, and how Jesus and John are connected in the same mission, as we saw in chapter 1. John is the last of the Old Testament prophets, and it was his job to point to the Messiah. All the people ***know*** that John was a great prophet, and that his authority came straight from God. And all the people knew also that he had pointed out this Jesus as the one greater than any prophet. So there shouldn't be any question at all about where Jesus' authority comes from, especially with all the miracles Jesus has been doing.

The leaders can't answer the question "Where did ***John's*** authority come from?" because they know that if they say, "From God" Jesus will say "Well why don't you believe what he said about me?" On the other hand, if they deny his authority from God, they were afraid of what the crowd might do or say, because the people had no doubt about John - he was a great prophet. So they wimp out, saying "we don't know", and Jesus knows, like the people know, that this is simply refusing to answer the question. So if they won't answer his question (when everyone knows what the answer is), then he won't answer their question (when everyone knows what the answer to this is, too). These smart, educated leaders end up looking like fools, like scared little children who won't stand up for what they believe in.

2. The Response

Jesus does have an answer for these hypocrites. He tells them a parable. When he tells the story about this farmer with a vineyard and the hired workers, he is really telling the big story about God 'planting' his people and leaving the religious leaders in charge. Like in the parable, God had spent a lot of time and energy 'planting' his people in the land of Israel. And like in the parable, God had many times sent his messengers - the prophets - to collect the 'fruit' from that work, and the leaders had, time and time again killed the prophets from God, only wanting to keep their selfish power to themselves and ignore God. Now at last, God has sent his own dear Son, and they are going to kill him too. The religious leaders get the point of Jesus' parable very clearly: "they knew he had told this parable against them"(v.12) and so they walked off, scared of the crowd who were probably thinking "Now let's hear you answer that one!" There is no hidden meaning in this parable - it's very easy for everyone to see what and who he is talking about. Jesus wonderfully answers their challenge about his authority by once again doing the job of a prophet, this time with words. It is very much like a prophet called Nathan once did with King David in the Old Testament. When Nathan told a parable about something bad the King had done, the king repented (2 Samuel 12). That's the way things were supposed to happen in God's kingdom. But the religious leaders around Jesus were not going to do that.

For us today, this is another great section in Mark's Gospel which helps us to appreciate what a ***big*** thing God has done in Jesus. When we read these stories, and look at the problems in our life and the world around us, we can think "It was all so long ago; God seems very far away; how can this change my life today? It all seems so ***small*** compared to the big world and the big problems around me." But it is not small at all. Try to imagine how big and impressive the temple was in Jerusalem. It was like Crown Casino, or the new Museum in Melbourne. If one of these buildings was suddenly destroyed by God, it would be a very big story in the news. And what if the Prime Minister was made to look silly on TV, not able to answer questions from a poor person on the news? And imagine if it showed the Prime Minister as a plotting murderer! That would be a very big story. Well it's like that in the story with Jesus and the religious leaders, but it's even bigger than that: It's the story of GOD coming into the world to bring very big changes; it's the climax of the long story of God with his people over 2,000 years before Jesus, and another 2,000 years since then. It's all very big, and very close, if we let this very real story into our hearts, to change us.

Reflect and pray: that God would help us see through the manipulation and lies all around us, especially coming from people in positions of power. Help us, Lord, to respond like Jesus did, with clarity and insight, with words of conviction rather than actions of violence. Help us to trust in your sovereignty, to know the comfort that comes from knowing your rule in our lives. Help us not to be people who strike out but rather lay down our lives in loving service for you. Help us to gain your perspective on things, to remain calm and deliberate in our witness, no matter what comes.

'Battle of Wits - Part II: Three Sticky Questions'

Read **Mark 12:13 -17**

This next part of the 'Town Hall Meeting' has the religious leaders again firing questions at Jesus. But unlike the previous question, which was a straight one about Jesus' authority, the questions now become sneaky, tricky ones, where the leaders can trap Jesus and have him arrested or thrown out of town. There are three questions, and this is the first one, about money.

Questions: Try to explain the logic of Jesus' answer.

Why is the question a tricky one?

What might the consequences be, if Jesus simply answered one way or the other, a yes or no?

Is Jesus only interested in saving his own skin with this wise answer?

How does his answer help us?

Who really owns the money and everything in our lives?

What sorts of abuses with money have you seen, both in cheating the government and unwise spending?

How has this passage challenged you about 'your' money?

The first thing to notice is the 2 groups of people who come to ask this question - the pharisees and the Herodians. These 2 groups would normally be against each other, since the pharisees followed God's law and hated others who had control of Israel, and the Herodians were friends of Herod, the Greek 'premier' who ruled in the area under the Roman supervision. For these two groups to be working together means something fishy is going on. The Herodians ***loved*** money, and would do anything to keep their power and keep the Romans happy. But the pharisees always preached ***against*** giving money to the foreign power of Rome; the coins had an image of Caesar on them, which was an insult to Israel's God who said, "You shall make no graven image, or worship it." The pharisees, when preaching from the Law, rightly put God alone as their ruler, not Caesar or Herod. But this is only what the pharisees ***said;*** what they ***did*** time and again showed that they, like the religious leaders of Israel in the past, were too often happy to go against God if it helped them hold onto their own power. The pharisees are just 'sucking up' to the Herodians, because it would help both of them to keep their power if Jesus was out of the way.

1. The Question

This question is made up just to get rid of Jesus. If he says "Yes, it's right to pay taxes to Caesar", then the pharisees would stir up the people - especially during Passover - to throw him out, because he would be saying the Romans are OK to rule over us. On the other hand, if Jesus says it's not Ok to pay these taxes, then the Herodians would drag him off and have him arrested for openly encouraging people to rebel against king Caesar. It's a sticky question, to which Jesus has an answer that keeps both sides 'happy' and stops them from doing anything against him. But more importantly, he goes to the heart of the question, seeing through their tricks and answering from God's point of view instead of just thinking about himself like they are. He answers in a wise way, as God would answer, and makes the Pharisees look like fools.

2. The Answer

Jesus' answer is especially good for us to work out our attitude to money. He says that money doesn't belong to us, but to the person whose head is pictured on it. This sounds really strange to us, but think about it - even in our day, the government makes the money at the mint, and then makes the laws which can bring back some of that money at any time to the government, through all sorts of taxes - income tax, petrol tax, gambling tax, cigarette & alcohol tax, sales tax, and now GST on almost everything you buy. Is the money really ours? Isn't it really what we end up with, in food, a home, clothes and health that are ours to keep, rather than the money? Even these are actually only on loan to us for a short time, while we live, and then go onto someone else when we die. Who really owns it all? God does. Jesus is giving us a good attitude to have with money. If the pharisees have become so obsessed with this question about money, then they don't know what really honours God. The money belongs to Caesar, so give it to him - it's only money - but your whole life belongs to God, so give that to Him. This answer from Jesus does give us a good guide about money, especially not to cheat anyone, even the government, but pay what they are rightfully due, and trust that God will give us everything we need, since everything is in his hands anyway. Trust God, not money.

It is amazing that even in the heat of a public argument with the religious leaders, Jesus is concentrating on helping our daily lives. He cares more about teaching the people than he does about protecting himself. Okay, for the time being these officials are kept from dragging him away in these incidents, but they are even more furious to get him - they'll be back. Jesus knows he is only making them more and more angry, but his love for the people (and us) is so great that he keeps doing his job right to the end. He knows how much money and concerns about money can chain us up and hurt our lives and the lives of our families. Jesus is telling us that we can indeed be protected from this destructive problem. If we don't have a lot of money, it is especially helpful to know that we will be alright if we trust God and don't try to cheat people. I have often seen people who try to cheat the government these days, especially with bosses who don't pay the right taxes for their employees and workers who work a second job for cash in hand, and even people on a pension who lie about their circumstances to keep receiving as much as possible. All of these are wrong, and we don't need to do it. All it does is fill us with guilt and fear about being caught. And it shows we are not trusting in God, being a good example to others, but we are trusting in our own clever corruption. Also it is not caring for the people around us who might genuinely ***need*** support from the government through taxes they collect; it just makes things harder for everybody. It is right to "pay to the Emperor what belongs to the Emperor."

There are also people who indulge in the way they spend their money. They get themselves into trouble financially and in other ways too, thinking that their money is ***their*** money, when in fact it is a living given to them by God. If you receive a pension or a wage, what does God want you to do with that? He wants you to do what is responsible for you and your family. He doesn't want you to spend half of it on alcohol, drugs, cigarettes or gambling. These things make your life more difficult because you run out of money, and they make your health go downhill. Think about it - do you have a right to treat your family and your own body like this? No. Your body and your children's bodies don't really belong to you, but to God who gave you life and blessed you with everything good in this world. You have a responsibility to look after yourself and your children, and to enjoy good health, and to ***enjoy life***. God really wants us to be free from the things that tie up our lives, but we must take our responsibility seriously. We must do our bit, and ***really*** want to change. We need to wake up to what Jesus is saying when he says, "Give to God what belongs to God".

Reflect and pray: Consider those areas in life that you find difficult to hand over to God, like money and control of your spending. Ask God to help you see the true value in everything he has given you. Ask Him to help you stop comparing what you have with what others have, and to be happy with that. Ask God to fill you with love for those you have responsibility for, rather than seeking more for yourself. Ask him to help you realize how much more we have in a western country built on Christian principles than 2/3rds of the world that live in true poverty. (and pray for them also!)

'Battle of Wits - Part III: The Second Sticky Question'

Read **Mark 12:18 -27**

The Sadducees were like many people today; they don't believe in a life after death like the Bible describes. They just look at the material things in life and say that's all there is. Some people might even believe in Heaven and God and angels, but they don't think it can make any difference to our life now, so they just concentrate on what they can see - "I'm sure everything will be alright after I die, God's so kind and loving - why worry about it?" So these people, like the Sadducees, only think about their 70 or so years on earth and try to make the most of it. And the Sadducees, like many of these people today, became rich, the 'upper class' in society, while at the same time being very religious, (they were like temple priests).

Questions: Why might the Sadducees ask such a question when they don't believe in the resurrection?

Is this a dangerous question, where the answer might get Jesus into trouble? Who is it designed to stir up?

What does Jesus mean by v.25?

Why is there no marriage in Heaven?

Will there be sex in Heaven and the resurrection? Why (or not)?

How does the title "the God of Abraham, Isaac & Jacob" show that God is the God of the living, not the dead?

Is the resurrection real? How do we know?

What ***is*** the resurrection, exactly?

How does all this affect your attitude to sexual relationships & marriage?

1. The Question

These Sadducees, like the other religious groups in the temple, also came to Jesus with a tricky question. It isn't a life-and-death question for Jesus, like the Pharisees had asked earlier. Rather it's a question to test whose side he's on - theirs or the Pharisees, because the Pharisees believed in the resurrection and the Sadducees didn't. It's also the sort of question they would throw at the Pharisees to make them look silly. It's a trick question where they think there is no good answer if you believe in the resurrection. And so they are asking it to make Jesus look silly too, just to stir up trouble in this 'Town Hall meeting'.

But it ***is*** a ***cleve***r question that goes like this: Everyone accepts that if a husband dies, then the wife is free to marry again. Now if this happens to a wife or a husband once, twice, any number of times, then in the resurrection who will they be married to? It's important to note that what they are all talking about when they say "resurrection" is not some airy-fairy spirit floating around in the clouds stuff. They all agree resurrection means our bodies coming back to life as real bodies in a real world. This is the life after death that the Bible teaches, and Christians believe in (especially after Jesus' body was resurrected and taken up to heaven).

2. The Answer

Jesus gives an answer in 2 parts. These are 2 strong answers to the Sadducees, that show he ***does*** believe in the resurrection, and they have got it all wrong. Maybe they thought he was going to side with them since the Pharisees had been giving him such a hard time, but no, Jesus plays no favourites. His answer contains 2 very helpful things for us in our lives today:

1) The Resurrection is real. This second part of his answer (verses 26-27) should give us great confidence that the resurrection is no fairytale, but is real. Jesus points out to them how God has called himself "the God of Abraham, Isaac and Jacob" in the Old Testament many times, and hundreds of years after these three had died. Jesus says that if these three people were only ever

going to rot away in the ground, then what sort of name is that for God to call himself? God is not a God of dust and ashes, a God of the ***dead***, but the God of ***life*** and the living. Why would he call himself that, if one day we weren't supposed to see him ***with them***? Their God is the powerful God of creation, so why would he leave the ones he loves rotting in the ground? God hasn't made ***you*** to end up rotting in the ground forever, either, but to be with him in a perfect and real world after this one, where there is no more death or pain.

2) Our Relationships are changed (verses 24-25). The Sadducees think a resurrection world would have to be just the same as this one. But of course they don't believe in a resurrection, so they haven't really thought about it. They don't understand that when we live in the unshielded presence of God, in the glory of God, this will change our relationships with people around us in a big way. We won't be looking for encouragement and comfort and company from people like we do now, because we will have those things directly from God. In marriage and sex, a person fully accepts and gives themself to another person, feeling a great, deep love where we are joined to another person. We won't need these things from people in the resurrection world, because they will be deeply met in a spiritual way that's 100 times better, directly from God. This is what Jesus means when he says we will be like the angels, with God face to face.

In our day it's hard to imagine anything better than our human forms of love, especially when we are continually bombarded with powerful messages of beauty and sex everywhere we look - on TV, computers, papers, posters, movies, magazines - everywhere. We need to realise how much all of this has been twisted into a false God in our western society. Sure, sex in marriage is good (actually I think it's great!) and a natural thing from God, but it's not perfect like our relationships will be in the resurrection. When we see Jesus and know him, we get a taste of this new quality of pure and faithful relationships, and points us to our new, permanent state in the future.

It's a great encouragement to us when we know that our relationships here on earth are not meant to be perfect, that the perfect will come after. This takes some of the pressure off us. The TV, social media and the world around us expect our relationships to be perfect - that's why so many people walk away from their relationships when things get tough. But we're not supposed to just walk away and keep looking for the 'perfect match' forever, to keep thinking only about the things we see and touch now. We're supposed to look to God for help, and expect that we can improve our relationships in ***God's*** way, looking to the things of heaven. So whether we're single or married we shouldn't be ***anxious*** about our relationships, thinking "I'd better get married soon, I'm 40 now!" or "I'm stuck with this person for the rest of my life!" We should be happy with what we have, never expecting ***too much*** from our relationships now, looking forward to the time when things ***will be*** perfect, and knowing we ***can*** also experience some of that comfort and joy direct from God right now, through Jesus. When we have this perspective, it's amazing how much more we ***enjoy*** the relationships we have.

Reflect and pray:

'Battle of Wits - Part IV: The Third Sticky Question'

Read **Mark 12:28 - 34**

The last 2 questions that have been asked in this 'Town Hall Meeting' have been nasty questions, trying to trick Jesus and have him thrown out. But this question is much more sincere; this Teacher of the Law who comes to Jesus has been impressed by Jesus' answers and wants to know what he really thinks. He asks a question that was a tricky one for all the religious leaders - they loved to discuss this question again and again, trying to find a good answer. They were often looking for a 'summary' of the Law, a short heading that was easy to remember, that covered all the teaching in the Old Testament. Jesus gave the best answer that has ever been given.

Questions: What do you think about this 'teacher of the law' - was his question a nasty one, like the previous two questions?

Why would anyone want to identify the most important commandment?

Why is Jesus' answer so good?

When the man responds again in v.32-33, Jesus is very impressed. What does Jesus mean when he says, "You are not far from the Kingdom of God"?

Is the Kingdom of God a place, or something else?

How do we get close to it, or enter it?

How do you feel about letting the King of the universe ***rule*** in your life?

What sort of reign is it? An oppressive one? What benefits are there?

How do we let him rule in our life?

The Greatest Commandment

One thing we find when we get close to Jesus is we get close to God. The Pharisees and Sadducees who asked nasty tricky questions of Jesus were very far away from Jesus; they kept their hearts and minds 'at arm's length' from him, and from God. But this Teacher gets very close to Jesus, asking a genuine question and appreciating the thoughtful answer Jesus gives. The question "What is the most important commandment?" is like asking Jesus "What is the most important thing about your relationship with God?" Straight away Jesus thinks about love. He knows very deeply that this is what God - his Father - is all about. Lots of people in Israel at the time of Jesus had their view of God blocked, and their hearts crushed, because the teachers always presented God as a God of laws, standing over them with a big stick. Sure, God gave commandments and laws, but not to beat people into submission. Jesus knew that even in the Old Testament, the true motive for obeying God is love. God had loved his people so very much, and he wanted their love in return, and he wanted them to be loving towards each other. That's what the laws showed them how to do - how to love.

What Jesus says here is the most wonderful summary of the commandments ever. Jesus puts two parts of different verses together, to make one. One part comes from Deuteronomy, and the other part from Leviticus. These are 2 of the 5 books of Moses at the beginning of our Bible, and these 2 are filled with laws. It's amazing that from these two books what comes to Jesus' mind are the verses about love. It's also amazing that Jesus put these 2 verses together - no-one else had ever done that. "Love God with all your heart, and love your neighbour as yourself" is also a neat summary of the 10 commandments, where the first 4 commandments are about our relationship to God, and the other 6 are about loving our neighbour. All the questions from the bystanders stop after Jesus says these words - they are just so amazed at his wisdom. Jesus certainly is the closest person to God, who understands what God is up to.

Getting close to the Kingdom of God

This Teacher of the Law seemed to take in what Jesus said in a deep way, and praised Jesus in front of everyone, even explaining why he agreed with Jesus completely. Jesus then says something to him that's stunning - "You are not far from the Kingdom of God". What does he mean? Think about it for a while before you read on - what do you think he means when he says, "You are not far from the Kingdom of God"?

Does he mean "You are a clever boy, who is getting closer and closer to the Kingdom of God, just keep it up, work hard, and you'll get there one day'? or does he mean 'You're about to step into a magical third dimension, the Kingdom of God - a spiritual world where you won't have to worry about this yucky world here anymore'? No, Jesus doesn't mean anything like this. The first example would be a person working his own way to Heaven, and the second would be just escaping from reality. Jesus is talking about something very real, very down to earth, but at the same time very spiritual, with power direct from God.

The Good News is all about the Kingdom of God coming to the world. That's what Mark's Gospel is all about. and this Kingdom comes in Jesus, the Son of God. This 'kingdom' (as we saw in 1:15) is not a place, but the living reign of God in people's lives. The Kingdom of God comes when the King from God comes to rule in your life, with all the wonderful blessings and power he has for us. So when Jesus says, "You are not far from the Kingdom of God" to this man, he is saying in effect, "You are not far from it, you are close to it, because you are close to ***me***." Lots of people got close to Jesus, but not with their hearts. This man's heart was close to Jesus, able to recognise the truth he spoke. This man's heart was ready to enter the Kingdom of God, was yearning to know God, open to God changing him.

Reflect and pray: Are ***you*** getting close to the Kingdom of God? Are you starting to ask questions from the heart, like this man was? Do you really want God himself to speak to you? Do you want to know the most powerful, loving person in the universe as your friend, the one who can really change your life? Then submit your life to Jesus, the King. He doesn't seek to dominate us, but to set us free from the things that oppress us, by the power of his life and his love. He makes us princes and princesses in his kingdom.

'Battle of Wits - Part V: Jesus Replies'

Read **Mark 12:35 -44**

All the people who wanted to question Jesus in this 'Town Hall Meeting' have been silenced by his answers. Now it's his turn, as winner of the debate, to make 3 closing points. Everyone has been impressed by his answers on points of the Law; he's obviously a very wise teacher. But now he tries to take them a step further, to understand that he is 3 things: the King much greater than King David, the Prophet who judges false religion, and the Friend of those who practice true religion. He is pointing to three different roles and relationships he has with people.

Key Questions: How would you describe Jesus' relationship/position/role with these three people:

He is David's............
He is the religious teachers'................
He is the poor woman's.............

Do you acknowledge (or even realise) these three roles Jesus has in his relationship with you?

Which ones do you accept more easily than the others? Why?

Can we ignore any one of them? How big is your Jesus?

What was it about David that put him in the right sort of position/attitude with Jesus (and God)?

What was it about the teachers that put them in the wrong sort of position/attitude with Jesus (and God)?

What about the woman?

What is the right way to worship God? And the wrong way?

Considering what Jesus says about the teachers, what should you expect of your pastors?

What would you do if you thought they were off track?

1. The King (v.35-37)

The Teachers of the Law have asked Jesus some tricky questions, now he has one for them. If the Messiah (the king they were expecting to come) was a descendant of King David, who was king 1,000 years before Jesus, then how could David call him "Lord" in Psalm 110? In their minds, a descendant was never greater than the father, but Jesus is pointing out that David has seen something special in a vision of the future: "The Lord (God) said to my Lord (the Messiah): Sit here on my right-hand side" The Messiah is much greater than King David. Sure, Jesus is indeed descended from King David, by his adopted father Joseph, but Jesus knows he is more than this - he is also God's Son. He wants people to realise how in the Old Testament there were clear signs of just how great their new king would be. They kept thinking about a king in merely earthly terms, who would be a warrior to kick out the Romans. But no, the coming King would be far greater than that, a king over King David even, and sit in Heaven at the right hand of God. They need to understand this, especially as Jesus is headed for the cross very soon, and would be raised from the dead and finish up just where this Psalm said he would finish up: at the right hand of God, as King of the universe!

How big is your Jesus? There were thousands of years of God's preparation for Jesus to come, and even the great king David called him "Lord". Is Jesus ***your*** Lord? Yes, he is - he is Lord of all the earth, whether you like it or not. Will you worship him as Lord, and trust in him, as the Good King who can give you life and blessing forever? Or will you ignore him, refuse to see him, like the Teachers of the Law did, and be judged, punished, destroyed by Him on the last day?

2. The Judge (v.38-40)

These days it's not a popular thing to accept God as our judge. People like to hear about God's love, but not his judgement and punishment of sinners. It's funny that at the same time, people in our world are demanding more and more justice from the judges in our courts! People ***do*** know what justice is, especially when someone has wronged ***them***; why is it so hard to believe that God also demands justice when we have wronged ***him***?

Jesus warns the crowd to be careful, to watch and see that they do not follow bad leaders, who make a big show about being religious, but don't live a Godly life. Those leaders will be punished severely by God, but those who follow them will be punished too, because they went after bad leaders. Jesus wants to save them from this. Israel all through their history had many more bad leaders than good ones. Jesus comes as the better leader than anyone else, and we need to measure our leaders against Him. If our Christian minister is wandering away from the truth, or living a life that brings dishonour to God - as we know these things from the Bible - then we have to do something about it. We need to check out what is right and say something about it - we don't just follow along. These words from Jesus are especially important for me, as a Christian minister, to hear. What God has given me to do is not something that's mine, but his. I must teach and live with great seriousness about God's will, or I will be judged with even greater harshness.

3. The Friend (v.41-44)

This poor woman is an example of what it means to honour God as Lord and follow the truth of his teaching. She knows how God sees everything and looks after those who truly trust in him. Unlike the rich people who were throwing in the leftovers of their pay, she put in all she had. What she put in was more valuable to God than what they did, and so Jesus expresses a sort of friendship towards her. He says in effect: 'Be like this - this woman really honours God; this is what it means to follow me.' What about you -

do you give God the 'leftovers' - both in the plate on Sunday, and with your time during the week - or do you give God the ***best*** you have, ***all*** you have?

In a way, all three of these little teachings are about true worship. The Jews were obsessed with getting their worship just right, in the Temple. But Jesus shows they have got it all wrong. They don't worship God in a right way at all. True worship is seeing God's great Son who alone can bring us into right worship of God. True worship means 1) bowing before Jesus as our only Lord, letting Him have the say in every aspect of our life; 2) following the truth as taught by Godly ministers; and 3) offering everything we have to God's service, not selfishly holding back. Lots of people in our world think worship is not very important - it's daggy and old fashioned. But all of us in fact worship something, whether it be our work or money or a house, a car, their physical appearance when they look in a mirror, sex, music, sports heroes, family, the stars, eastern philosophies - you name it - no human being worships nothing. But only worship of the true God will avoid God's judgement and death - worshipping his wonderful Son who gives us life and blessing and forgiveness of sin.

 CHAPTER 7 

Life on the Line: final warnings and preparations with the disciples

'Last Things'

Read **Mark 13: 1 - 13**

This is only the second large block of teaching from Jesus in Mark's Gospel. The first was back in chapter 4, where Jesus taught about faith and the Kingdom of God. Here in chapter 13 is his last major body of teaching, preparing his disciples for the struggles to come upon them after he's gone. He wants them to know he's coming back, but in the years before he returns, circumstances will become tough for Christians. He wants them to understand that the ***world*** they live in may not be changed all that much by his death and resurrection, but ***they*** will. It will be hard for Christians, not easy, but they can hang on if they understand what is going on and don't give up their faith.

Questions:

Why do you think God destroyed the temple (in 70AD), just as Jesus predicted? What are the good things and the bad things about having a temple?

Why has this Jewish temple never been rebuilt again?

What do you think is Jesus' purpose in telling his disciples (and us) about the terrible times ahead?

What sort of things have we seen in our time, from his list?

What is your response to people who get worked up about predictions of the end of the world?

What does God want our response to be, when things get tough(er)?

What would you do if your family turned on you (v.12)?

1. The Temple

The temple was a sign to Israel about God being present with them. It was the place where God's shining light would come down into the holy place. But time and again God brought judgement on the people and destroyed the temple. People became too proud and superstitious about it, thinking that if they just defended the temple then they could sort of 'keep' God with them. Well God is not a god to be kept in any building, the God who made the universe. And when Israel kills their Messiah, the temple is soon after destroyed again, both as a sign of God's judgement, and a sign that

God has done something new. In the year 70 AD, the temple is completely destroyed, just as Jesus predicts here in v.1-2. And to this day, it has not been rebuilt. Never before had God left his temple in ruins for so long. As a sign for the old Israel, the destroyed temple shows they are under God's judgement, for killing God's Son, as Jesus predicted in chapter 12. But God is also doing something new. No more temple is a sign that God is no longer worshipped in a temple of stone. When Jesus dies for our sins and is raised to life forever, a new, open worship of God is made possible for all people everywhere. No more temple is a sign of God's blessing going out beyond Israel, to all the world. People are now able to worship God "in Spirit and in truth"(John 4:23). The new temple is Jesus' own body (John 2:19-21).

2. Prophets and Politics

In the days after Jesus' death and resurrection, many false prophets will come, he says, and lots of disturbing events in the world like earthquakes and wars. What are we to make of this? Jesus says "***Don't be troubled***" by it. There are people around these days who get terribly troubled by these things, and they're not listening to Jesus. People get hung up on predicting dates for the end of the world, and trying to identify the returned Christ, and stirring up panic among people. We are not supposed to get worked up over this. Jesus tells us these things so that we are ready for them to happen, so that we're calm, and it's no surprise. In our day, these sorts of things have happened a lot. We have seen the David Koresh doomsday cult in Waco, USA. We have seen terrible earthquakes, floods, bushfires, volcano eruptions, and many wars. More people have died in wars during the last 100 years than in any other century.

Even though these terrible things make us sad, seeing so many people suffering, we are supposed to have a quiet, calm, and even an encouraged attitude towards it all. Why? Because these are signs that the end is getting closer. Is that a time of terror for us who are Christians? No, because it's a time of getting closer to God's finish of things, where all evil and suffering will come to an end, and God's people will live in peace forever. Jesus wants us to understand all of this, so that we can continue with peace and faith and confidence in God, no matter what happens. These things are not supposed to shake us off balance. It's not as if things have gone wrong in God's plan. They are actually signs that things are on track in God's plan. So when you see people getting all worked up about these things, and trying to scare you, tell them how wrong they are, and how their fear is a sign of their lack of faith in God. If they won't listen, then have nothing to do with them unless you are very strong to keep challenging them.

3. Holding firm under persecution (v.9-13)

As time goes on, things will get harder for Christians, even in our western world. Like in Jesus' day, and the years of the first Christians, people don't like being told they are wrong, and governments are becoming less tolerant of people who value truth more than money. A time is coming when we will be persecuted because we do not bow to money like the world does. Jesus speaks to his disciples in their time, telling them "You will be arrested... you will be beaten.... put to death..... Everyone will hate you because of me." And he is also saying this to people in our time; many people will suffer these things as we get closer to the end. What are we supposed to do? Fight? No, Jesus says to speak, and be guided by the Holy Spirit in how we speak. This strong persecution may never happen to you or me in our lifetime; it comes in more subtle ways. But the lesson is the same: don't be ashamed to speak of your faith, in the face of abuse from anyone. Sometimes our own family can be the hardest source of pressure for us to give up our faith, or change what we do into something unchristian. Jesus says don't even be surprised about this (v.12). Again, Jesus wants us not to be worried, but to simply hold firm, knowing that these sorts of things are supposed to happen.

Reflect and Pray:

What sort of dazzling things might attract you, and lead you away from true faith? Beautiful buildings, like in v.1-2? Or money and possessions, maybe?

How hard is it to trust in Jesus instead of these things?

What nice ***teachings*** might attract you away from true faith (like in v.3-6)?

What ***politics*** might attract you? (v.7-8)

What ***emotional*** ties attract you? (v.9-13)

What are we supposed to do, when tempted by any of these influences?

'Last Things' (2)

Read **Mark 13: 14 - 37**

This is the hardest part of Mark's Gospel to understand. Jesus keeps going with his description of the 'last things', the 'end times' before Jesus returns. There are terrible things that will happen before the end, and Jesus wants his disciples to be ready for it, and he wants us to be ready too. He tells it in the same way the Old Testament prophets did, where the words they say are fulfilled in the time of the people who heard them first, but also fulfilled at a much later time in an even bigger way. This is the key for us to understand Jesus' words; to see how these things have partly been fulfilled for his first disciples, but then also look forward to our own time.

Questions:

When are "those days"(v.17,19,20)?

Who is in control of the end of the world?

How does that make you feel?

What is "the awful horror, standing where it should not be"(v.14)?

What does Jesus want us to do, in these troubled times?

What does his title "Son of Man" (v.26) mean?

What sorts of false prophets have we seen in our day?

How should we respond to them?

1. Terrible signs of the End (v.14-27)

The first sign Jesus tells them about is the "awful horror standing in the place where it should not be". It's a bit mysterious; Mark doesn't explain it for us, but keeps it hidden, saying "let the reader understand". This awful horror is something we should be able to work out, but Mark doesn't want to spell it out. It all makes sense if we look back at the history of what happened about 40 years after Jesus said these words, in 70 A.D. The Romans surrounded Jerusalem, destroyed the temple, and nearly wiped out all the Jews and Christians living in the whole area. The words 'awful horror' could be translated "desolating sacrilege", that is, some horrible, obscene thing is set up in the temple that desecrates it, that makes the holy place a dirty place. This is what did happen when the Romans destroyed it. The soldiers rode through on their horses with their helmets and flagpoles with images of eagles and the emperor on them (which is banned in the first commandment). When Jesus uses these words and Mark says, "let the reader understand", they are remembering a time about 200 years before, when the Greeks had taken over the temple, and sacrificed pigs on the altar, and set up a statue and a temple to the Greek god Zeus right on the temple site. The prophet Daniel, another 200 years before that, had predicted this desecration, using almost the same words as Jesus did. So Jesus and Mark understand that this sort of thing is going to happen again, and does in 70A.D. It is quite clear this is what Jesus is talking about. Mark probably doesn't want to be too clear about it because he doesn't want anyone to be arrested with a copy of his Gospel and then punished even more by the Romans. When all of this terrible chaos is happening, the disciples are to flee, without looking back, or they will be wiped out. But it's also a warning for our time. The places and the things we might regard as sacred will be destroyed - so don't hold onto them. Even today, the temple site has a desecrating thing built on it - the Islamic Dome of the Rock. This stands as a sign to us that the End is still on the way, getting closer every day. Jesus wants us to be ready, to hold onto the one true faith in God.

In our time false prophets have also come, like Mohammed, like Joseph Smith (Mormons), like the Jehovah's Witnesses, David Koresh, and many more. Don't be shaken by these, because none of them change God's plan for us, and Jesus told us these things would come (V.24-27).

2. Know the Time but not the date (v.28-37)

The exact date when the end will come is not important - that's up to God, and even Jesus doesn't know it. What is really important is that we understand that the End ***Time*** has come. It's like extended time, or penalty time in a football match, right at the end, full of anticipation that it will soon be over with the winner declared victor. We can see the signs of the end all around us, and we should be encouraged to hold onto our faith, knowing that God is bringing evil and sin to an end. So when you see people getting hung up on the date when Jesus will return, don't follow them, because they are paying more attention to a date than to their faith in God. We are supposed to see the ***signs*** of the Time, like we see the new growth coming on the fruit trees and know that summer is coming (v.28-29) but not worry about the date. We are supposed to have faith in Jesus and his words, which "will never pass away", rather than putting our faith in dates. I am sure that if everyone knew the exact date when Jesus was to return, then everyone would turn from their sins and put their faith in Jesus one week before that date. But God doesn't work like that; he only wants genuine faith, not false faith, so nobody will know the date. We are supposed to be ***ready***, so that ***whenever*** the end comes, we are not surprised by it (v.33-37).

3. God's Chosen People

Notice how three times in this chapter Jesus calls his people God's "***chosen*** people". This is a great encouragement for us, because it tells us about how special we are to God. If God has chosen us, then nothing can separate us from him, not "trouble, or hardship, or persecution or hunger or poverty or danger, or even death.... there is nothing in all creation that will ever separate us from the love of God which is ours through Christ Jesus our Lord", as St Paul says in Romans 8. So when we do face troublesome times, as Jesus is preparing his disciples for, we need to remember we are God's chosen children, and he ***will*** look after us and strengthen us, if we hold onto him in faith.

4. The Son of Man comes (v.26-27)

The overriding encouragement of this section is the fact that the end will be ***God's*** end, not just some mistaken human cataclysm or natural disaster. The end comes with the return of the Son of Man on the clouds. This is the first specific reference to what Jesus means by his title 'Son of Man'. Up to now, it has been a sort of disguise, equal to 'mere mortal', but now, near the end, it becomes clear what he really meant all the way through: he is fully human, yes, but he is also the heavenly being from God. Here his words are so close to those from the Old Testament prophet Daniel, chapter 7, which is a vision of the end, where "before me was one like a son of man, coming with the clouds of heaven.......his authority will last forever, and his kingdom will never end"(v.13-14). This title is also in the same way picked up by John in his vision of the end in Revelation (1:13; 14:14). This is an immense encouragement, that the end of time is in Jesus' hands; he will return as king and judge, and for us his children there is nothing to fear and everything to gain at that time. He wants us to be "on your guard"(v.23), "on the lookout"(v.33), "keeping watch" (34,36), so that none of these troubling signs take us by surprise or put us off balance, but keep us focused on the good ends that God has for us in Christ Jesus.

Reflect and pray: Lord Jesus, help us to keep our eyes on you when things get rough. Help us to know your comfort and guidance, provide us with wisdom and insight so we might stand firm rather than giving in to fear. Help us to know your guaranteed end for us, in the glory of a new creation without pain or evil, filled with love and peace.

'Final Actions'

Read **Mark 14: 1-26**

Jesus' final teaching is over, in chapter 13, preparing his disciples for the time when he is not around anymore. Now it's time for final actions. It's not so easy to remember a bunch of words someone has said to you, but these actions will make a lasting impression on the disciples' minds. After Jesus' death and resurrection they will powerfully understand what Jesus' death was all about.

Questions:

Think about the woman with the perfume. Can you think of any reasons why she did this?

Is the protest from the disciples reasonable?

Does Jesus' response indicate that he doesn't care about the poor?

What does the woman's action indicate, even though she most likely didn't realise it?

Do you have any thoughts on why Judas betrayed Jesus?

What is the significance of the Passover, when it comes to the timing of Jesus' death?

This is the first time the word 'covenant' has been used in Mark. What did the bread and wine signify when celebrating the old covenant associated with Passover (in the Exodus event way back with Moses – see Exodus 12)? What are the parallels with the new covenant and Jesus?

1. The Authorities Prepare for Action

The timing of everything is done to perfection in the events of these last 2 days, as scene after scene builds up to the final climax. Timing is crucial, for Jesus to finish off his time with his disciples just the way he planned. And so the Jewish authorities are held at bay for just a little longer, until the big festival of Passover is finished. Jesus has some room to move, for just 2 more days. He ***wants*** his death to be as close as possible to Passover, because the Passover itself will explain his death. This great annual festival is charged with emotion and strong national feeling for the Jews. There are probably 2 million people in Jerusalem. If there was even a hint that the Messiah had arrived, during the Passover (as many Jews believed he would), then there could be absolute chaos, even rioting, which would be met with brutal force from the Roman guards whose numbers were increased for the festival. The Jewish authorities understand this situation very well, so they wait tensely, plotting the final details of how to arrest Jesus as soon as the festival is over.

2. A Final Act of Love (verses 3-9)

To the very end, Jesus is the friend of outcasts, the unloved, the people looked down on by society, and now eating in the home of a (now healed) leper called Simon. And in an emotion-filled scene with no words spoken, a woman comes up to Jesus' feet as he and his friends are lying on the floor around a low table. There are no words, but I can imagine the eyes of this woman meeting Jesus' eyes, and the deep understanding and love between them. What was this intense, unspoken communication all about? Answer another question and it becomes clearer: Where did she get an alabaster jar of this most rare (probably from India) and expensive perfume? And why did she have it in her possession anyway? Because she was most likely a prostitute, and a good one, an elite Mademoiselle, not just a street walker. No words are needed.

This act of ***breaking*** such an expensive item - worth a year's wages for an average worker ($70,000 in today's terms) - this is a powerful act of breaking her ties with her past life, leaving it all behind, pouring it all down the drain. But better than that, she pours it on Jesus - changing her shameful wages into beautiful blessing. She pours out the proceeds of her life as a sign of true love for the one man who had obviously shown her true love at some time in the past. One man had refused to treat her as a sex object but as a person, understanding her feelings of being lost and full of shame, and her desire to be a whole person again, a person who could hold her head up in public with dignity. Here was the one man who offered her life back - and could give it back.

On top of all this, she is unaware of just how significant her action is. Jesus tells his disciples that her action is a further sign of his coming death. She is preparing his body for burial ahead of time. Again the timing of things is significant; there will not be time straight after Jesus' death to anoint his body (see 16:1). But also, consider how all of this is ***God's*** timing in moving this woman's heart to do this lovely thing 'just in the nick of time', as a strong sign and a strong example to the disciples. This woman's action was a truly great act of love, repentance, sacrifice, significance, and faith in Jesus. And Jesus is absolutely correct in predicting that this will be known all over the world, as we now have it in Mark's Gospel.

3. Judas Goes into Action (v 10-11)

In stark contrast, an act of great love and devotion is immediately followed by an act of greed and treachery. As God moved the woman to break down, Satan finally got to Judas and moved him to break out, giving in to his love for money and his frustration that Jesus was hell-bent on dying instead of raising an army like the Messiah was supposed to. Judas' opportunity to be a commander beside the King was slipping away. So he may as well get what he can out of this hopeless situation and help the Jewish authorities. This is a dead-of-the-night cloak-and-dagger scene, where the lurking traitor is revealed to us, the audience, but not to the disciples.

4. The Final Action of Jesus (v.12-26)

Jesus has his own final action which has been planned well in advance (v13-15). His act is an act of fellowship with his friends. It is also the last meal of a man headed for execution. And it is filled with meaning, left for all disciples that follow thereafter as a permanent explanation of what his death is all about. The Passover meal was a great celebration about what God had done for Israel over 1000 years before in the time of Moses. The Pharoah of Egypt had refused to free the 600,000 Israelites who were his slaves. So one night God told Moses he would send the 'Angel of Death' to strike down all the first-born sons in the land - even Pharoah's son. But in order for Israel's sons not to be killed, each household was to kill a lamb and splash some of the blood over the front door, so the Angel of Death would see it and 'pass over' that house. In this way the lamb died instead of the first son. The family was to then cook and eat the lamb quickly, because Pharoah was going to kick them out as soon as he realised Israel's God had killed his son. God ordered Israel to celebrate every year this powerful act of God, where he saved his people from slavery (See Exodus chapters 11-12).

Jesus' death is closely connected to all of this. On the night that Jesus celebrated this meal, there would have been about 200,000 lambs killed, one for every 10-12 people, or per family. Masses of blood would have totally covered the altar in the temple, where the lambs had to be killed. The people learned from this the serious life and death situation they were in if it wasn't for God. As the life ran out of the lambs, God promised life for the people. It was like renewing a contract each year - a contract which had been signed in blood on that first night. This contract was called a covenant - a special contract where God and the people pledged their loyalty to each other and God promised his love and blessings for the people (they had the best end of this contract!). Jesus gives this meal a new meaning, one that fits exactly the pattern of the old meaning, but makes it much more powerful and effective. He indicates that after this meal, the ***bread*** they were eating would symbolise his body which was going to be sacrificed, just like the lambs. And the ***wine*** they were drinking would symbolise the blood he was going to pour out for them. He was replacing the lambs. In the same way that giving up their life brought life to the people, so would Jesus, but in a much more powerful way. His death brought about a new covenant, with all people, whereby people's sins would be forgiven and the personal, loving blessings from God would be poured out like never before. No longer would there be any need for animal sacrifices, because the death of God's lamb, God's Son, would have incredible power forever. And hence, in the act of commemoration from hereon there is no lamb involved, the bread now represents the body instead.

The last point to note is how Jesus is fully aware of what is coming. He deliberately, willingly, goes ahead to his death for us. He knows about Judas but doesn't dob him in. By Judas going ahead with his plan, Satan thinks he is winning, by killing Jesus. But Satan is in for a big surprise and disappointment, where he will be left powerless after Jesus' death. No-one is compelling Jesus to die, except God. He could have escaped at any time, he ***could*** have taken control of Jerusalem if he wanted to - he is the Son of God. But God's plan was to sacrifice him, for him to win over death itself, in order to break the curse of death hanging over all of us. But if Jesus was going to represent all of us on that cross, he had to go freely, without force, in obedience to his Father in order to undo all of our disobedience. He is God's Son who has ***come to show us God's love for us***. His mission is to willingly sacrifice himself in order to save us from death and slavery to sin - what an act of love!!

Reflect and pray: It is worth contemplating over and again the enormous, earth-shattering change Jesus' death has made for the world. Thank the Lord for this precious gift of fellowship time in what we now call Communion or the Lord's Supper. Such a huge sacrifice with huge repercussions has unending depth of meaning motivation for us. Sit in this for a while, soaking up the love of God for you and his world.

'Three Desertions – The Truth emerges'

Read **Mark 14: 27 - 52**

In the previous section, final preparations have been made by all the key players - the Jewish authorities, the disciples (through the woman), Judas and Jesus. Now the moment has come. And it is a moment of mass defection. Jesus will take his final steps to the cross utterly alone. Despite their assertions of loyalty even to death, his friends will all desert him at the time when he most needed their support. It is a ghastly scene, as suddenly, in a few brief moments of sheer panic, the seriousness of the situation finally dawns on his disciples and they run away, leaving him to die.

Questions: What word(s) would you use to describe these scenes?

How do you think Jesus felt when his friends deserted him in his time of prayer and at the arrest?

Why doesn't he run away himself? Would he have preferred to avoid what was coming?

Where in your life is "the spirit willing, but the flesh is weak"?

Do you think the court hearing is a proper one, or a 'kangaroo court'? Why?

Could Jesus have talked his way out of it? Why didn't he?

What is it that eventually gets them to convict him?

What do you think of Peter, in this section? Why did he deny knowing Jesus?

What does God do, when we fail badly, like this? What does he want us to do?

Are you encouraged, or discouraged by Peter's failure? Why?

1. Peter's Desertion Predicted (v.27-31)

As with many other scenes in Mark, Peter is held up not as the greatest of the Apostles, but as the greatest fool, the one who is always ready to open his mouth and say what he feels, but then he's made to eat his words. Every time, except for one, he gets it wrong. He is the prime example of the disciples' misunderstanding about Jesus and what was going on. He is only saying what all the others were thinking, and in this case, also saying (v.31).

Like with Judas, Jesus knows what Peter will do. Jesus has an amazing awareness of what is going on in people's hearts, and more than that, he is a prophet, he can see ahead to what will happen. Jesus describes precisely how and when Peter will deny that he even knows Jesus. But Peter cannot bear the thought that he could possibly do such a thing - his love and loyalty to Jesus, his closest friend, is 100% - he is so sure that fear will not overcome it. Peter is like most of us - able to make wild promises among friends, but when it comes to the crunch, we so often put our own safety first. At the end of his three denials, he is personally crushed by his inability to hold firm, and breaks down in tears. It's amazing that in the face of such a terrible failure, Jesus later restores him (see John 21:15-17). This is a real encouragement for us, that no matter how badly we fail sometimes, Jesus can forgive and restore us.

2. Deserted in Prayer (v.32-42)

Jesus goes to the one place where he can find the strength to go on - he goes to God in prayer. He is a real human being, and in great fear and torment he prays, asking God to "take this cup of suffering away from me". He is terrified of what is coming and asks for a way out. And it is not just fear of pain and death, it's fear of being cut off from God for the first time ever. And it's also a fear of losing his friends; even now, on the eve of his death, they still don't understand, won't stay awake and pray - are they ready for what is coming? Will this all be a waste? Has he prepared them well enough, so they don't lose faith after his death? These must be some of the tormenting questions going through his mind. To the last, Jesus is concerned for his friends. He wants them to pray for themselves, that they will not be tempted to give up their faith (v.38).

Even with all this fear and uncertainty, there is one thing Jesus is sure about - God knows what he is doing, and God has been moving everything to this very point. What is most important to Jesus is that God completes his plan, and that Jesus obeys God's will in this. So Jesus adds to his prayer, "Yet not what I want (make happen) but what you want." Jesus knows very well that God only answers prayers in a way that is in line with his will. And so, under great stress, Jesus stays on track. He knows that no matter how much he might suffer, he is prepared to do it for the ones he loves, because that is God's plan; there is no other way.

Added to this stress is the greatest disappointment, the deepest sadness at his friends, these ones he loves so much, deserting him like this, not praying with him in his time of need, but nodding off to sleep. "How could they sleep at a time like this? By this time tomorrow I'll be dead! And any minute now I'll be taken away!" They just could not believe what he had said about dying. They had seen all the power of his words and his miracles. "Surely nothing could kill him if God was with him so strongly."

3. Deserted Completely (v.43 - 52)

Jesus' last moments with his disciples are distressing. Moments before, his friends could not stay awake with him; now they would not stay with him at all. In the dead of night, the temple police and a crowd tagging along for some excitement barge into the sad but silent garden. Ignoring the group of disciples sleeping, they are focused on arresting just one man - Jesus. And in the darkness, it was important to get it right. So Judas, who had led them to the garden, had also arranged a signal for them. When he was close enough to see Jesus clearly, he would betray him with a kiss. A kiss was the customary way for a student to greet his teacher, his Rabbi. To do this for the purpose of arresting Jesus is particularly sick.

Things happen quickly. The guards grab Jesus. Someone grabs a sword and hacks off a guard's ear. Then in panic everyone scatters. Finally, a very young man, probably Mark himself, is almost grabbed. He might have charged to the scene from his house in Jerusalem to warn Jesus, after being awakened by the passing crowd, just wrapping his sheet around himself. It's as if Mark is putting his signature here by saying "I too was there, and I too abandoned him."

Horribly alone, Jesus is now in the hands of his enemies who will kill him. Right up to a moment before, he could have run himself. But now the opportunity had passed. In the middle of this scene of chaos and panic, Jesus stands still, firmly resolved to go all the way in obedience to his Father. The only calm person in all this mayhem, he keeps the situation from getting out of control, by reminding the guards that they could have taken him at any time; he wasn't going to put up a fight. There was no need for force. Jesus knew that it was all supposed to happen this way, even with the disciples scattering. "The scriptures must come true", as he had read it in the Old Testament, the Hebrew Bible.

CHAPTER 8

His Time Has Come

'True witness, False witness – the Truth Obscured'

Read **Mark 14:53-72**

The very end of Jesus' life is as filled with as great a variety of relationships as any other part of his life. Deserted by his disciples he is 'thrown to the wolves', yet things continue to go according to plan. A long list of different people are yet to play their part in a rapid succession of significant relationships with Jesus.

And there is a pattern - from low reluctance on the part of Pilate, rising to heated despising and hatred by the crowd and the soldiers, then down to a deep, dreadful recognition by one soldier, rising to brave loyalty by Joseph and then up to the unbelievable heights of surprise by the women at the tomb on Sunday. These last hours are a rollercoaster ride of tragedy like the world has never before seen. It is electric, where the heavens and earth are shaken to the core, and the air is thick with the awesome attention of God. Attention fixed on the greatest, most heartbreaking deed God had ever been involved in - the death of his own beloved Son.

Questions

Does this 'court' case look like proper proceedings?

Why do you think Jesus stays quiet throughout most of this 'court' case, instead of defending himself?

How can God sit by and allow such injustice? Doesn't God care?

What do you think v.62 is really referring to? Why is this hugely important?

Why do you think Peter acted the way he did? In what way is he an example for us?

What should we do when we are tempted to minimize or hide our faith in Jesus?

Deserted by Justice (v.53-65)

All that remains is the 'kangaroo court', the setup trial in the dead of night, which was designed to trap him in a web of false evidence. If it wasn't so serious, it would be funny, because try as they might, they could not get their evidence to agree. They could not find a charge to pin on him. In the end, Jesus had to help them out. It is only when he answers their question about him being the Messiah, that finally they have something. All the false witness against him is only successful once Jesus makes a true witness about himself, about who he truly is. Talk about going all the way, willingly!

This is his second clear identification with the "Son of Man coming on the clouds", a prophecy about Jesus from Daniel 7. But Jesus looks and acts nothing like what they expected from that passage in Daniel. They are offended at the implication he could be that 'Son of Man' because he is not acting like a warrior who will kick out the Romans and restore the greatness of Israel. What might a modern person in our time think of this situation Jesus finds himself in? We might expect, as a climax to the whole story, an 'L.A. Law' style outcome, a fiery court scene where the innocent man walks away untouched because of a brilliant defense. But instead we have a huge disappointment, a total flop. The innocent man puts his head on the chopping block. How on earth can this be the mighty Saviour of the world, God Almighty himself, when he submits to this horrendous abuse at the hands of liars and despots? How could God possibly put up with this? Surely he would slay them on the spot! But no, we must be patient like God is patient, taking his time to work things out just perfectly. This is all God's will, where the totally innocent, pure, perfect sacrifice of his own Son is the only answer to the problem (sin) he came to solve. The truth will come out, but only after the real culprit has well and truly hung himself. The surprising outcome that demonstrates God's justice (see Romans 3:22-26) will send shockwaves around the world to change millions (or billions?) of lives for eternity. And the ultimate justice is coming in the end, when we all face Jesus as judge, as we saw in chapter 13, with some declared innocent and some declared guilty.

Another False Witness (v.66-72)

It's one thing for your enemies to lie about you; it's another when it's a close friend. Although Jesus didn't hear the words Peter spoke, he had predicted them. Jesus feels the weight of both forms of false witness against him as he sits before the authorities. Such an affliction of utter desertion of justice and support is probably beyond anything we will ever experience. The hammering he gets in psychological and spiritual terms is in line with the physical beating at the end of these proceedings.

Peter's denial is meant to be a solid example for us as followers of Jesus. Think for a minute about the purpose in the mind of one of the disciples writing this account in the first place. It paints a very negative picture of Peter, who had become the head of the church soon after Jesus is taken back up to Heaven. Why tell us these details, when they make the church look so weak and ineffective? It's one of those instances where the honesty of the account is important for the writer. Peter gives us the model of what it is like to be put on the spot, made to give an account of our faith, even under the threat of death. If Peter had owned up, he most likely would have been crucified along with Jesus. Peter has even said earlier that he is prepared to do this. But when it comes to the crunch, he can't go through with it. Fear takes hold. How often does this same dynamic affect our witness today? Is it fair to our Lord, that we should be ashamed of him when the going gets rough? We need to recognize that we have two big advantages over Peter: we have the whole story, including a full understanding of the meaning of Jesus' death and resurrection, in the New Testament; we have the Holy Spirit living inside us, poured out after Jesus' death and resurrection. Peter had neither of these things at the time.

Reflect and pray: that we would find strength in those times when we feel sorely oppressed, under the pressure of society to comply with their standards instead of God's standards. Help us to give a better account than Peter did, as we have opportunity to witness about our faith, with the help of the Holy Spirit.

'Cowardly Sentence, Courageous Sacrifice'

Read **Mark 15:1-32**

Even in the harshest, most difficult times, Jesus keeps relating to people. He knows each one's hearts in this string of encounters on his last day. Instead of complaining, protesting, demanding justice, he meets each one with the appropriate attitude, knowing full well that all of this is happening according to God's plan. Jeus allows each one in this sad procession to play their part.

Questions

If you had been there, which group might you have been part of? The officials, the crowd, the soldiers or the criminals?

Think about the weaselly ways of both Pilate and the Jewish authorities. Why are their 'processes' so very wrong?

Where is justice in these scenes? Is this a fair trial?

How can the crowd be so against Jesus here, when only days before they welcomed him into Jerusalem like their king?

Why do you think Mark does not hold back in telling us the horrible details of Jesus' crucifixion?

Jesus and Pilate: Pilate is the Roman governor of Judea. He has great powers and he is answerable to Caesar, the Roman emperor. He didn't particularly like the Jews, because they were influential people who made things hard for the Romans sometimes. He wanted to keep the Jewish leaders happy as much as possible, because this made things quieter and more peaceful for him, since the Jewish system had their own laws which were good for keeping the peace in the region. But the Jews knew who was boss, and Pilate wanted them to feel his power whenever possible, so that they didn't forget it. One thing that showed them this was Pilate's power to order someone's death. If the Jews had convicted someone under their law where the sentence was death, they had to bring those charges and prove them to Pilate, and he would have them executed, if he agreed with their judgement. This is what happened with Jesus. The Jews wanted him dead, and so they held a trial with their council and the teachers of the Law. But this was a hurried thing, done early in the morning so it didn't attract too much attention. It was an illegal trial under Jewish Law, and Mark doesn't even call it a trial, but just a meeting where they made plans. When they brought Jesus to Pilate, he quickly saw that things were not right. He had been through this sort of thing before with the Jews, and he knew what the right process was. They were supposed to bring witnesses and prove their case convincingly. The only thing they accused him of was claiming to be a king, which under Roman law was punishable by death. But there seemed to be not much against Jesus in their case. If there were witnesses, they must have been very unconvincing, and it was very strange to Pilate that Jesus said nothing in his defense, except a short "You say so" when asked if he was the King of the Jews.

Jesus doesn't deny the charge, because it is true; he ***had*** claimed to be the Messiah, the King from God. But the point of the story is that he did not get a fair trial under the Jewish Law, nor was there enough evidence to execute him under Roman Law, and Pilate says this himself (v.10,14). Both the Jews and the Gentiles ***murdered*** him even though he was innocent of any crime. Pilate, with all his power, tried to talk them into letting him go, but in the end was weak, just wanting to keep them happy. When pushed, they are terrible lawbreakers, all of them, who don't really value life and justice. They represent all people of the world, all of us, Jews and Gentiles, who sent Jesus to the cross because of our sins. And in his relationship with Pilate, Jesus keeps quiet, even though he could have defended himself and got off the charge. Like the Old Testament prophet Isaiah predicted "He did not open his mouth; he was led like a lamb to the slaughter"(Isaiah 53:7).

Jesus and the crowd: Who were this crowd, who demanded Jesus' death? How could it be that the people of Jerusalem who a few days before welcomed him into the city with shouts of "Hosanna" could now want him dead? It could be that this was a 'rent-a-crowd', which the Jewish leaders had gathered specially for the occasion, but it doesn't seem quite like that. This was an annual event, where people would gather for the public release of a prisoner (v.9). It's in this atmosphere that the chief priests exert their considerable influence with the people, "stirring them up" to release a rank criminal instead of Jesus, and to demand Jesus' crucifixion. So the crowd have a part in this, where they too share responsibility for his death. They are just like people everywhere who often have the chance to vote on some serious issue, and end up following bad advice, or giving in to complacency, saying "I don't really know what's going on here, all I know is I have to vote". Does this excuse them from the decision they have been part of? No it doesn't. It's important for us to see here that the crowd represents all of us. We all are responsible for Jesus dying on that cross, whether we're aware of it or not. Our sins are effectively our 'vote' against God, are the cause of him hanging there on the cross, and if any one of us were in the crowd that day, we would have been calling out "crucify him" with the rest of them.

Jesus and the soldiers:_These are the ones who are hired to do the dirty work for everyone else. They're the only ones who actually lay hands on him - flog him with a whip that rips your skin off, push a twisted wreath of thorns onto his head, beat him over the head with a rod, spit on him, mock him, then tie him to a cross, and for good measure belt nails through his wrists and ankles, and lift him up to hang there, for all the world to see. These are the brutes who inflict pain, but they only do it because it's their job; no one else has the stomach for it. They even mindlessly dress him in a purple robe just for fun, the garb of a king; there are bullies in every age. Jesus dies for them too.

Jesus and Simon:_Simon of Cyrene is the odd one out; he's a complete foreigner just passing through, ignorant of what's going on, roped in to do some heavy work, as the Romans were used to making black slaves do. He's just a lowly innocent bystander who's forced to become part of this violence. He doesn't understand anything that's going on - but Jesus dies for him too, because like everyone else, he also has sinned in his life, against God.

The passers-by and the Jewish authorities (v.29-32) Talk about kicking a man when he's safely pinned down! These are like vicious young hoods are sometimes, after a few drinks, or like some adults who never really grew up. "Aha! What a phony! Come on big boy, let's see you work your power now! Can't, huh? 'O look at me, I'm the Son of God, king of the universe! I can bring the dead back to life!' Well can't you come down off that cross, if you reckon you're so great? Come on, let's see it!" Jesus died even for them, who are most violently opposed to him; even they are not impossible to save.

Jesus and the 2 criminals:_These are the ones who really deserved death. Here they see a man dying horribly, in the same boat as they are, and they hurl insults at him. Of all the people, you would expect these two to have some pity on him, but no. That Jesus dies with these two is significant - he dies ***with sinners***, he is reckoned with sinners. From the beginning at his baptism right to the end, he is identified with sinners, right down to the very worst of us, taking the due sentence of death for us, even the lowest scum.

Reflect and pray: Just how easy is it to get sucked into the ways of the 'crowd' these days? Pray for insight and wisdom to follow God's lead instead of giving into sin like just about everyone in these scenes did. And pray against self-pride, where we become blind to our own wretchedness, thinking ourselves better than others when the truth is, we're just as bad as anyone else. Daily pray 'forgive us our sins, as we forgive others'.

'Truly Dead. But not Gone'

Read **Mark 15:33 – 16:8**

Questions

It is time for the biggest questions, the most important questions in Mark. There are only four that in the end really matter.

Did Jesus really die?

Why did he die?

Did Jesus really rise from the dead?

If everything he said and did during his 3 years of ministry displayed the truth about God and humanity, love and sin, (that is, Mark's account of these things is believable and accurate) then he died and rose again, then what are the implications for your life?

Jesus and God

Here we see how the tragedy of God meets the tragedy of humanity, to save it. This is ***the most significant*** relationship in this unfolding drama, the relationship between the Father and Son. This is the most significant relationship in the ***universe***, where God and his son have lived in an unbroken relationship since before the creation of the world. When Jesus dies here, he is really dead - cut off from God for the first time ever. When Jesus cries out those words from the cross, they indicate his relationship with God is truly separated**.** That was the plan; his relationship with God is broken so that our relationship with God can be mended. This cosmic suffering and expulsion from God connects with our hopeless suffering and expulsion from God, in order to transform it into glory. His temporary separation from God restores our permanent separation from God. See how serious our sins are, that God would go to such lengths, where the only remedy that would have any real effect was God's own Son, dying in our place. In Mark's Gospel more than the others, we are meant to ponder this, long and hard, sitting with the power of his death, before rushing on too quickly to his resurrection.

Jesus and the army officer:_Finally, there's a faint glimmer of recognition from one of the many standing by. Just one man, a toughened officer, sees the way Jesus dies, in the face of all this abuse, calling out only to God. This hardened officer is deeply impressed, touched by the realisation that "this was indeed the Son of God". He probably means no more than "***a*** son of God", but in the same way as the woman's actions, who earlier unknowingly prepared Jesus' body for burial, this man's words are, unknown to him, a significant prophetic word, where God has moved him to say just the right thing at the right time. This man stands as the model for us and all the other people in this scene. We must recognise who it really is, hanging on that cross, if we are to be saved by Jesus' death. And this man begins the trend of such a recognition spreading to the Gentiles. It is interesting to note that the title "Son of God" is only used here and in the first verse of Mark's Gospel, forming 'brackets' around the whole thing; what Mark asserts in the first verse, people must come to recognise by the end; we must ***see Jesus*** for who he really is.

Jesus and Joseph: Here at last is one of the Jewish officials who has become a disciple of Jesus. (John tells us Nicodemus was there too - John 19:39). It is not impossible for highly educated, influential, wealthy people to see the real Jesus, it just happens less frequently because of the lure of such things, living a comfortable life most don't want to give up (as we saw in 10:17-27).

The Sign of Hope (16:1-8)

Jesus and the women: This last scene finishes Mark's Gospel on a very familiar note: They were "alarmed"(v.5,6), "terrified...afraid"(v.8). These women have not ***seen*** him yet, in his resurrected state, just like we haven't. What will they make of this report of his resurrection? Was his death a failure? This is the sort of question millions of people have pondered over the past 2,000 years, with a variety of answers, mostly negative. Mark has thought about the situation we might find ourselves in, where we don't have the benefit of seeing Jesus in the flesh, in his resurrected body. So Mark finishes his account abruptly, before the women have a second chance to recognize Jesus, along with the other disciples (as the other Gospels show us happened). We are left with a scene that matches our own experience. We haven't seen him in the flesh, but we are challenged to see him for who he really is, in our minds, our hearts, our soul. The living Jesus can touch us spiritually in the here and now, to confirm the truth of these things. What do you make of it? Do you require visible proof of his body, to believe? Or have you experienced his invisible presence, by faith, as you have read Mark's account?

One last point. Do you remember way back in 4:38 I made the point about the cushion Jesus was sleeping on, how such an irrelevant point encourages us about the first-hand nature of the account? The involvement of the women as the first witnesses to Jesus' resurrection works in a similar way. Many people today claim that the resurrection of Jesus was concocted, a lie spread by the first disciples. But the straightforward, honest way Mark tells us about the witness of the women speaks against such a view, because they were women. In that culture of the time a woman's witness was not regarded as anything valid. If you were going to make up the resurrection of Jesus, the last thing you would do is rely in your story on the witness of women. Nobody would believe it. The truth about Mark's account is confirmed not on the basis of the sex of the person giving witness but by the lives that are changed forever after the day of Pentecost, when the Holy Spirit is poured out into the lives of those who believe in Jesus (see Acts chapter 2). There is no need for any part of the account of Jeus to be made up, because the truth is testified through the direct action of God in the life of a person who puts their trust in Him. In short, the truth of everything about Jesus' life and death is proven by his resurrection and the truth of his resurrection is confirmed by the Holy Spirit. It's God's work through and through, not the work of any mere human. You can 'see' Jesus today, because he is alive and active. Praise the Lord.

Reflect and Pray: The truth of everything Jesus said and did was confirmed by his resurrection. He died for our sins, but without any sins of his own, therefore he couldn't stay dead. Pray that the hope of a whole new life will inspire you and billions of others to keep going in life, knowing that the future is not futile but guaranteed for all those who put their faith in Jesus the Saviour, the Son of God.

APPENDIX

A note about the ending of Mark's Gospel.

Many people have tried to reconcile the extra verses found in some of the early documents of Mark. Your Bible might continue on as normal through to verse 20; my NIV only includes those verses 9-20 as a footnote. One of the things that gives us great confidence in the validity of the New Testament as we have it today is the way we can research so many documents that have survived through the ages. These original documents were written in Greek, which was the most common language across the trading world at the time, like English is today. One document was discovered in 1859 in a monastery at the foot of Mt Sinai in Egypt. This document contains most of the books of the New Testament, and **this document** was written in the early 300's, which means the parts, each book within it, were written perhaps 50 to 100 years before that. It is this ancient document, called Sinaiticus, which ends Mark's Gospel at 16:8. There are others also that end Mark in the same way. There are also other documents that add part or all of the verses to verse 20. To cut a long story short, the evidence is quite clear that this section from verses 9-20 were added at a later date and are not part of the original Mark. The vast majority of ancient manuscripts that do include these verses are dated later than Sinaiticus.

Do such discoveries lessen our confidence about the accuracy of the New Testament? No, quite the opposite. That thousands of ancient copies of the original text are available from all ages all around the world, for anyone to see, shows the openness that churches through the ages have had towards transparency, despite there being some differences between some documents. The vast majority of differences are small and inconsequential. They are nearly all explained by a simple human error when copying an older text. And most of those can be explained by a dictation being misheard by the scribe. But some changes are obviously deliberate (there are only a few of these, however), like this ending of Mark. All of these variations can be looked at in special compilations that every theological college relies on (see below under *Acknowledgements*). Nothing is hidden.

The question is why would someone think it necessary to add this ending to Mark's Gospel? The answer is that it felt incomplete, lacking the resurrection confirmations in Matthew, Luke and John. If Mark's Gospel is the first one written (and it almost certainly was), then some years later when the other three started circulating, it would look to some people that Mark was incomplete. But by that time, many copies of the original Mark would have been copied and circulated (and kept being circulated in this form, for centuries to follow). Hence the discrepancy. No conspiracies, no manipulation or hidden church agendas. Just complete openness for anyone to check out for themselves. Given this openness and vast array of early texts, the New Testament is known to be the most reliable, verifiable ancient text of all time. Discussion about this ending of Mark actually gives us grounds to have the highest confidence about the accuracy and reliability of everything that comes before it.

ACKNOWLEDGEMENTS

I need to acknowledge **various people** who have helped me in writing these studies over the years. First and foremost is the Revd Dr Peter Adam, who was the Minister in Charge at St Jude's Carlton when I worked there as Minister to the Housing Estates. Pages could be written about his patience and persistence, encouragement and wisdom in dealing with someone as rough and troublesome as myself. It was Peter's suggestion that I write my own studies on Mark to use with the folk on the Housing Estates.

I owe a great deal of thanks to those people living in the public Housing Estates in Carlton. Although I tried my best, I know I failed in many ways to serve them as they deserved. I will always remember with fondness both residents and volunteers who helped: Geoff, John, Elaine, Phil, Alfred, Patricia, Tri, Duc, Long, Royce, Kim, Shan, Tam, Dung, Ron, Patrick, Lucy, Sally, Rose, and a host of others whose names have become in my mind dim with age, but I still see you.

Huge thanks go to my wife and children, who put up with a lot over the years.

The parishioners at Holy Trinity, Bacchus Marsh and St. Luke's Mulgrave, who supported and encouraged me so much in ministry.

Various colleagues who have encouraged me over the years, including Peter, Lance, Noel, Charles, Bert, John, Andrew, Ken, Mark, Blake, Harley,

Steve and Toby, and especially dearly departed David Williams my gold-rolled Greek and New Testament lecturer from Ridley College Melbourne.

Some of the resources used (there have been many over the years, some of which I have forgotten, but here are the ones I still hold).

Mark Commentaries

- William Barclay, *'The Gospel of Mark'.* Saint Andrew Press, Edinburgh. 1954 and 1971
- Augustine Stock, *'The Method and Message of Mark',* Michael Glazier Inc. Delaware, 1989
- James Morison, *'Commentary on the Gospel According to St Mark',* Reprinted 1981, Klock & Klock, USA. Originally published by Hodder and Stoughton, London, 1884.

The Greek New Testament, Eds Aland, Black, Martini, Metzger and Wikgren, with the Institute for New Testament research. 3rd edition, United Bible Societies, 1983

ABOUT THE AUTHOR

Paul M. Harper is a retired Anglican Pastor, born in 1961. He has been married for 45 years, with two natural daughters and one foster daughter with disabilities. He lives in Ballarat, Australia. He loves the Bible and has spent more than 20 years preaching and teaching in study groups. Beginning at St Jude's in Carlton as Minister to the Housing Estates, then in Bacchus Marsh, Mulgrave and Ballarat, his passion for down-to-earth explanation of the rich contents of God's Word has never wavered. He recoils from lofty, over-educated studies, preferring a straightforward style in everyday language that presents the truth in uncomplicated but accurate ways. God's word should be easily accessible to all, even with people who don't read much. In Martin Luther's words, Paul wants the 'plain sense' of the text to shine through.

Paul grew up in a Roman Catholic family in Melbourne. He went through 12 years of Catholic education and became a chef after training at the Melbourne Hilton. At the age of 28, his life was changed through a radical conversion to Christ. He then studied for five years at Ridley Theological College, Melbourne. His other interests include fishing, camping, watching motor racing and AFL football, He has also published a science fiction novel titled *Tentacles, Night of the Machines*.

Other books written by this author

Tentacles, Night of the Machines, Green Hill Publishing, 2025

This new take on Science Fiction does so with Christians in mind, answering the question 'If aliens do exist, would they know God?' Without the usual sex, swearing or murderous intent of usual sci-fis, this one you can share with friends and family.

To get in touch with the author please email him at paulharper50@gmail.com

www.ingramcontent.com/pod-product-compliance
Lightning Source LLC
LaVergne TN
LVHW050635100826
845148LV00011B/1874

* 9 7 8 1 7 6 4 3 8 2 0 9 0 *